DARE TO BE
Different

DARE TO BE *Different*

A DEVOTIONAL ON **LOYALTY, INTEGRITY, AND THE SOVEREIGNTY OF GOD** IN THE BOOK OF DANIEL

SHERWOOD PATTERSON

 QUEST PRESS

Dare to be Different: A Devotional on Loyalty, Integrity, and the Sovereignty of God in the Book of Daniel

Copyright © 2024 by Sherwood Patterson

Published by Quest Press
a ministry of Quest Church San Diego
All Rights Reserved
P.O. Box 2111
Alpine, CA 91903

www.QuestSD.com

Printed in the United States of America

All rights reserved, no part of this publication may be reproduced, stored in a retrieval system, or transmitted in any form or by any means - for example, electronic, photocopy, recording - without prior written permission of the publisher. The only exception is brief quotations in printed reviews.

All Scripture quotations, unless otherwise indicated, are taken from the New King James Version ®. Copyright © 1982 by Thomas Nelson, Inc. Used by permission. All rights reserved.

DEDICATION

TO the extraordinary congregation of Quest Church, your insatiable hunger for God's Word is a radiant testament to your profound commitment to spiritual growth. It is with immense gratitude that I dedicate this book to each of you, acknowledging the humbling privilege of walking alongside such dedicated seekers of truth. Shepherding and teaching the Bible within this community is a sacred journey, and your fervent passion and collective pursuit of Christ have enriched our shared exploration of faith in ways beyond measure.

INTRODUCTION

WELCOME to a transformative journey through the captivating narrative of the Book of Daniel, an 80-day devotional designed to unravel the threads of fearless faith, daring devotion to God, and courageous spiritual character that defined the life of this extraordinary biblical figure. Daniel's narrative serves as a timeless testament to what it means to be different as a faithful follower of God in the midst of a world often at odds with our biblical beliefs.

Daniel's unflinching faith stands out as a shining example, challenging us to emulate his resilient commitment to God in the face of adversity and trials. The Book of Daniel not only unveils heroic stories of faith that inspire, but also delves into prophecies of future revelations. These visions emphasize the sovereignty of God over earthly powers and ultimately reveal the redemptive plan of salvation through Jesus Christ as the promised Messiah and eternal King of kings.

Beyond unraveling the Book of Daniel's key events, themes, and verses, this devotional aims to bridge ancient wisdom with modern life, offering practical applications for contemporary challenges. It is my sincere hope and prayer that through these reflections you will not only gain a deeper understanding of the Book of Daniel, but also be challenged to take bolder steps of faith for God. May this devotional inspire you to dare to be different in our culture, embracing dedicated loyalty, growing in spiritual integrity, and submitting to the sovereignty of God in every aspect of your life.

Sherwood Patterson

Day 1

THE HEAVENLY CONDUCTOR

"In the third year of the reign of Jehoiakim king of Judah, Nebuchadnezzar king of Babylon came to Jerusalem and besieged it. And the Lord gave Jehoiakim king of Judah into his hand."

DANIEL 1:1-2

IMAGINE a grand orchestra poised on a stage, instruments in hand, each musician ready to contribute their unique sound to a symphony that will resonate through the hearts of those who listen. At the center of it all stands the conductor, guiding the flow of music, harmonizing diverse tempos, and intimately knowing every note. The conductor weaves each component together, creating an inspirational masterpiece that captures the soul. Much the same way, God, as the heavenly conductor, divinely orchestrates human affairs into His masterful plan.

The story of Daniel begins in a tumultuous era of Israel's history — a time when the nation faced the heavy hand of divine judgment due to their persistent idolatry and disobedience against God. The Babylonians, led by Nebuchadnezzar, laid siege to Jerusalem, eventually taking captive the people of Israel. At first glance, this may seem like a tragic defeat for God's chosen people. However, as the story unfolds, we discover that God not only foretold these events but also used them for a far greater purpose.

In fact, Isaiah had prophesied about this judgment long before it came to pass. In Isaiah 39:6-7, we find a prophecy regarding the exile of Judah to Babylon. The fulfillment of this prophecy underscores the reliability and consistency of God's Word. What God speaks through His prophets is bound to unfold, confirming His authority over the affairs of humanity. These events serve as tangible reminders that the accounts in the Bible are not mere myths, but are indeed records of real people and real situations. While the instruments of God's judgment may be striking, they are wielded by the hands of the ultimate conductor.

God is firmly in control when our lives are full of chaos.

Remarkably, in the tragedy of Israel's exile, God was at work, using painful circumstances to fulfill His divine plan. Looking back at Israel's experience, we are reminded that God is firmly in control when our lives are full of chaos. Just as God turned the brokenness of Israel's past into a beacon of His goodness, we have the same assurance that He is actively working in our lives as well. Romans 8:28 assures us that God works out all things for the good of those who love Him and are called according to His purpose.

In times of uncertainty, we are encouraged to place our concerns into the loving and capable hands of the heavenly conductor. Just as the conductor brings order to the symphony, God brings order to our lives. Trust in His sovereignty, knowing that He can turn the chaos of your circumstances into a beautiful masterpiece that aligns with His divine purpose and plan. Embrace the truth that our heavenly conductor is always at work, weaving the threads of our lives into a symphony that glorifies His name.

Day 2
DARE TO BE DIFFERENT

"But Daniel purposed in his heart that he would not defile himself with the portion of the king's delicacies, nor with the wine which he drank; so that he might not defile himself."

DANIEL 1:8

IN the construction industry, there is a fascinating process that takes place when working with concrete. In its fluid state, concrete is poured into wooden forms, structures raised to control and manipulate the substance as it hardens. These forms determine the shape and purpose of the final product. In a way, our lives are like concrete, constantly being molded and shaped by the influences around us.

Making up your mind to do what's right in the moment starts by settling the matter first in your heart.

Consider Daniel, a young man taken into captivity in Babylon. Much like the construction process, he underwent years of training, not by wooden forms, but by the cultural and social influences of Babylon. In the midst of these pressures to conform, Daniel refused the king's portion of delicacies because it went against his biblical convictions. In this seemingly mundane act, Daniel dared to be different, to stand out from the crowd, and to uphold his commitment to God. There was too much at stake to just stay silent.

Certainly, for Daniel, making a big deal out of a little meal wasn't an easy or rash decision. Especially since defying the orders of the most powerful king in the land carried with it extremely dangerous consequences. However, while Babylon sought to shape Daniel's behavior, God had already prepared him for this moment by forming his character. Daniel demonstrated courage when faced with the king's decree, boldly distinguishing himself as different from his peers.

As Christians, we face similar pressures in our culture – pressures to compromise our convictions, to conform to practices or beliefs that contradict God's Word. Just as a concrete forms determine its final shape, our choices shape our character. That's why making up your mind to do what's right in the moment starts by settling the matter first in your heart. Daniel's example not only inspires us to be courageous, but also challenges us to be rock solid in our convictions, regardless of the potential consequences or final outcomes.

Daniel's bold stance encourages us to examine our lives. Are there areas where we might be defiled in our hearts towards God? Are we allowing the world to shape us instead of standing out for the Lord? In a world that often pushes conformity, dare to be different. Resolve to stand firm in your convictions, to let the Word of God shape you instead of conforming to the ways of the world. In doing so, you will find that God will honor your commitment to be set apart for Him.

Day 3

GOD'S DIVINE GUIDANCE

"Now God had brought Daniel into the favor and goodwill of the chief of the eunuchs."

DANIEL 1:9

PICTURE yourself on a vast, open sea, navigating a sailboat through ever-changing winds and currents. In this metaphorical journey of life, we often find ourselves facing challenging circumstances where it feels as though we're at the mercy of unpredictable forces. Daniel's life in Babylon serves as a powerful analogy for how divine intervention can transform our course, guiding us when we surrender control to God.

As Daniel stepped onto the shores of Babylon, he was like a sailor entering uncharted waters. He was a foreigner in a foreign land, immersed in a culture that sometimes contradicted his deeply held beliefs. The Babylonian court, with its customs and expectations, was a turbulent sea of influences that could easily have overwhelmed him.

Yet, Daniel remained steadfast in his commitment to God. He was like a sailor who, amidst the changing winds, steadfastly held onto his anchor. In surrendering control to God and trusting Him as his divine Navigator, Daniel found himself moving against

The best way to let go of control is to take hold of God's guidance.

the current of Babylonian culture and into the favor and goodwill of the chief of the eunuchs.

This divine intervention in Daniel's life wasn't merely a matter of luck or chance, it was the hand of God directing his course. Just as a skilled sailor adjusts the sails to harness the wind's power, Daniel adjusted his heart to align with God's will. He found himself sailing on the divine wind, carrying him to places he could never have reached on his own.

Similarly, in the midst of life's stormy uncertainties, the best way to let go of control is to take hold of God's guidance. Just as a sailor relinquishes control of the boat's course to the prevailing winds, we too must release our grip on circumstances and trust in God's divine plan. He places us exactly where He wants us to be His ambassadors, even in the midst of challenging and unsettling seas.

In your own journey of life, consider the winds and currents you face. Are there situations where you need to surrender control to God, trusting in His guidance and divine intervention? Remember that God can bring you into favor and goodwill, not by your own effort but through His power at work in your life.

When confusing circumstances surround you, seek God's direction and trust in His divine intervention. Just as the sailor relies on the wind to reach the desired destination, trust in God's leading to guide you to places of influence and impact. Surrender control, set your course with faith, and let God's divine wind carry you toward His purposes, where His favor and character-building work await.

Day 4

REFINER'S FIRE

"Please test your servants for ten days, and let them give us vegetables to eat and water to drink."

DANIEL 1:12

HAVE you ever seen a skilled blacksmith working in his workshop? He begins by heating a piece of iron in the blazing fire until it becomes red-hot and malleable. Then, with precision and care, he shapes it into a strong and beautiful tool. In this process, the iron undergoes a transformation, from a raw, unrefined material into something valuable and purposeful.

Similarly, in the fiery furnace of life's trials and challenges, God often uses times of testing to increase levels of trust in Him. Daniel's decision to request a diet of vegetables and water amid the sumptuous feasts of Babylon serves as a powerful analogy of how our faith is strengthened over time.

Just as the blacksmith subjects the iron to intense heat to remove impurities and strengthen it, God occasionally allows us to face difficult circumstances to refine our faith. These trials are like the furnace's flames, designed to purify our hearts and minds.

Daniel's choice demonstrated remarkable courage. He could have been filled with fear for disobeying the mighty king, punished severely for his actions, or felt a deep sense of loneliness in a foreign land. Yet, he leaned into this challenging situation, just as iron submits to the refining fire.

As the iron in the blacksmith's fire is transformed into a useful tool, our faith, when tested, is shaped and strengthened. James 1:2-4 puts it this way: "My brethren, count it all joy when you fall into various trials, knowing that the testing of your faith produces patience. But let patience have its perfect work, that you may be perfect and complete, lacking nothing."

In the midst of life's trials, remember that God is the Master Blacksmith. He skillfully hammers away impurities, molds us into vessels of honor, and equips us for His divine purpose. Trust in Him as Daniel did, knowing that these testing moments are opportunities for God to refine your faith, producing in you steadfastness, godly character, and a radiant hope.

God often uses times of testing to increase levels of trust in Him.

Embrace the refining fires of life with courage, for it is in these trials that your trust in God is tested and your faith becomes not just a belief but a tangible reality. Just as the blacksmith creates something beautiful and valuable from raw iron, God transforms us into vessels of His grace and instruments for His kingdom. Your trust in God, once tested and refined, becomes a beacon of hope and a testament to His faithfulness for all to see.

Day 5

DEVOTED TO GOD

"To these four young men, God gave knowledge and skill in all literature and wisdom; and Daniel had understanding in all visions and dreams."

DANIEL 1:17

IN the midst of a culture that often celebrates conformity, Daniel stands out as an inspiring example of how God-honoring convictions can lead to God-given blessings. Daniel's story is a testament to the profound truth that a life wholly dedicated to God can thrive even in the most challenging and compromising circumstances.

Daniel and his friends had every opportunity to immerse themselves in Babylonian society and forsake their devotion to God's commands. However, despite their immersion in this culture, they remained immensely holy to God's ways.

Although fully immersed in the world, we can remain immensely holy to God's ways.

Daniel's journey was marked by a remarkable balance. He received excellent secular training, excelling in literature and wisdom, but not at the expense of acquiring godly traits. This balance illustrates a powerful principle for us as believers: it is possible to excel in the secular realm while maintaining unwavering commitment to God's principles.

The image that comes to mind is that of a tree. Just as a tree firmly rooted in good soil can bear abundant fruit, Daniel's life, deeply rooted in God's truth, produced extraordinary wisdom, knowledge, and understanding. He was like a tree that stood tall, providing shade and sustenance even in the midst of a dry and barren desert.

As Christians living in a world that often contradicts our faith, we may feel like exiles at times — surrounded by values and practices that diverge from our convictions. Yet, like Daniel, we can choose to remain dedicated to God's commands, knowing that His blessings will follow.

This passage reminds us that God is the source of all knowledge, wisdom, and understanding. He is the One who equips us to excel in every aspect of our lives, secular or spiritual. When we prioritize our relationship with God, when we seek His wisdom and understanding, He blesses us with knowledge and skill beyond our human abilities. In the face of lousy and dreadful circumstances, Daniel remained steadfast because he drew his strength from the Lord. Likewise, in the challenges we encounter, we can rely on God's strength to uphold our convictions and live for His glory.

Today, take a moment to reflect on your own life. Are there areas where you have compromised your convictions? Are you fully dedicated to God, seeking His wisdom and understanding in all aspects of your life? Remember that, just like Daniel, you can stand firm in your faith, excel in your endeavors, and be a light that shines brightly in the darkness of this world. With God's strength, you can live a life that honors and glorifies Him, even in the midst of challenging circumstances.

Day 6

SPIRITUAL THERMOSTATS

"Then the king interviewed them, and among them all none was found like Daniel, Hananiah, Mishael, and Azariah; therefore, they served before the king."

DANIEL 1:19

IN our daily lives, we often encounter two types of instruments that measure and impact the environment around us: thermometers and thermostats. While both have their purpose, it is the thermostat that holds the power to change the temperature of its surroundings. Likewise, as believers, we are called to be spiritual thermostats, not mere thermometers, in our culture.

Daniel and his friends exemplify this concept beautifully. They were not content to merely reflect the spiritual temperature of their Babylonian surroundings; instead, they had the power to change it. As they stood before King Nebuchadnezzar, they were found to be unlike anyone else in the kingdom.

A thermometer, when placed in a room, simply reflects the temperature that exists. It doesn't have the power to change the environment; it only tells you what it's like. On the other hand, a thermostat has the ability to set a desired temperature and work actively to bring the environment in line with that desired setting.

Daniel and his friends were spiritual thermostats. In the midst of a culture that often contradicted their faith, they actively worked to set a different spiritual temperature. They didn't conform to the pagan practices and beliefs around them. Instead, they stood firm in their commitment to God and His principles.

The world around us may sometimes seem overwhelming, and conforming to its ways may appear to be the easiest path. But remember, you cannot transform the world by conforming to its ways. It takes individuals who, like Daniel, dare to be different, who actively seek to change the spiritual climate.

> *One life wholly consecrated to God has the potential to create the most significant spiritual change in the least likely places.*

One life wholly consecrated to God has the potential to create the most significant spiritual change in the least likely places. Just as Daniel and his friends influenced the Babylonian court, you too can impact your workplace, community, and relationships. Your commitment to God's ways, even in challenging circumstances, can be a catalyst for transformation.

As you go about your daily life, strive to be a spiritual thermostat. Set a standard of godliness, integrity, and love for Christ in your surroundings. Do not be content to merely reflect the spiritual temperature of your culture, actively work to change it. Be an instrument of God's grace and truth, knowing that your influence can bring about spiritual transformation, even in the most unlikely places.

Day 7
GODLY RIPPLE EFFECTS

"And in all matters of wisdom and understanding about which the king examined them, he found them ten times better than all the magicians and astrologers who were in all his realm. Thus Daniel continued until the first year of King Cyrus."

DANIEL 1:20-21

HAVE you ever dropped a rock into a calm, still lake and watched as ripples spread outward, touching the water's surface far beyond the point of impact? In a similar way, Daniel's life serves as a beautiful analogy of how a faithful witness for Jesus can create ripples that reach far and wide, impacting generations to come.

Daniel and his companions were like that rock, dropped into the vast sea of Babylon's royal court. They were exiles in a foreign land, yet they chose to maximize every opportunity, relationship, and conversation for the glory of God. Over time, their faithfulness created ripples that went well beyond their immediate surroundings.

Just as those ripples in the lake extend outward, Daniel's influence spread far beyond the boundaries of the Babylonian court. He didn't just excel in his duties, he excelled ten times more than the most skilled magicians and astrologers in the entire kingdom. His faithfulness to God was evident in every aspect of his life, and it didn't go unnoticed.

Throughout his life, Daniel served under several Babylonian and Persian kings, including Nebuchadnezzar, Darius, Belshazzar, and Cyrus. In each of these high-ranking positions, he maximized his influence and boldly witnessed for God. His integrity, wisdom, and devotion to God had a profound impact on the hearts and minds of those around him, including powerful kings.

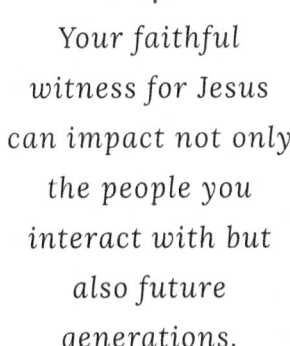

Your faithful witness for Jesus can impact not only the people you interact with but also future generations.

In your own life, consider the pond of your workplace, family, and relationships. You, too, are like a rock that can create ripples of influence for Christ. By maximizing your opportunities to be a witness for Jesus, you can have an incredible impact that reaches beyond your immediate sphere of influence.

Seeing your workplace, family, and relationships as places where God has planted you to bloom for Jesus brings incredible meaning and significance to the normal routines of life. Just as Daniel's faithful witness had a ripple effect, your faithful witness can impact not only the people you interact with, but also future generations.

Today, remember that you are an ambassador for Christ, just as Daniel was. Embrace each opportunity to share your faith and demonstrate godly character. Your influence, like those ripples in the lake, can extend far beyond your imagination, touching lives and leaving a lasting legacy for the glory of God. Be encouraged to be a bold witness, knowing that your faithful testimony can have a godly ripple effect for generations to come.

Day 8

TRANQUILITY IN CHAOS

"Then the king said to them, 'I have had a dream, and my spirit is anxious to know the dream.'"

DANIEL 2:3

CIRCUS jugglers are skilled with an extraordinary talent. They gracefully toss multiple objects into the air, seemingly defying gravity and chaos. In contrast, King Nebuchadnezzar's response in Daniel 2 resembled someone trying to juggle too many balls at once — resulting in irrationality, unreasonableness, and instability. I wonder if you can relate?

Imagine yourself attempting to juggle an increasing number of balls. As the number grows, it becomes challenging to keep them all in the air. The balls begin to drop, bouncing chaotically around you. In a similar way, Nebuchadnezzar's dream left him feeling overwhelmed, like a juggler trying to manage too many balls.

> God picks up our burdens the moment we lay them down to Him.

As a result, his spirit was anxious to know the dream's interpretation, and his response was far from measured or rational. He made unreasonable demands of his wise men, threatening them with severe consequences if they couldn't reveal both the dream and its meaning. His behavior became erratic and unpredictable.

But there's a better way to handle life's complexities — one that leads to tranquility in the midst of chaos. Instead of trying to juggle all our concerns and responsibilities, we can choose to lay them down before God. Life becomes overwhelming when we choose to carry the weights and burdens in our own strength. Just as a juggler would set aside the balls they cannot manage, we can surrender our burdens to the One who can handle them. There is no burden to heavy that God cannot carry.

Think of it as going to God with a jumbled handful of balls and handing them over one by one. As you entrust your cares to Him, He takes control, providing peace and stability in return. In Psalm 55:22, we are encouraged: "Cast your burden on the Lord, and He shall sustain you; He shall never permit the righteous to be moved." In 1 Peter 5:7, the Apostle Peter reinforces this eternal truth when he said, "Cast all your care upon God, for He cares for you." God's willingness to handle our concerns demonstrates to us His deep love and care for every detail in our lives.

When life's complexities threaten to overwhelm you, remember the skilled juggler who knows when to release the balls. Similarly, release your concerns to God, allowing Him to bring order to your chaos. Remember, God promises to pick up our burdens the moment we lay them down to Him. As you surrender your worries and responsibilities, you will find tranquility and stability, free from the irrationality and unreasonableness that can result from trying to juggle life's challenges on your own.

Day 9
EARTHLY WISDOM

"The Chaldeans answered the king, 'There is not a man on earth who can tell the king's matter; therefore no king, lord, or ruler has ever asked such things.'"

DANIEL 2:10

IN moments of distress and uncertainty, our natural inclination is to seek solutions and answers from the tangible world around us. King Nebuchadnezzar's response in Daniel 2 reflects this very human tendency. When faced with a troubling dream, his first instinct was to turn to worldly sources for answers, even though they were insufficient and incompetent.

Imagine you are parched and thirsty in a vast desert. You stumble upon a mirage, an illusion of water shimmering on the horizon. Desperate for relief, you hasten toward it, only to find it vanishes, leaving you still thirsty and disappointed. King Nebuchadnezzar's reliance on magicians, astrologers, and sorcerers was similar to chasing after mirages in a barren desert.

In this moment, the king sought an answer to a profound and perplexing dream, one that troubled his heart and mind. He placed all his hope and trust in the wisdom of those who claimed to possess supernatural insight, despite their inability to provide any real answers. None of Babylon's magicians could fathom the depths of the dream or its interpretation.

In our own lives, we often mirror the king's actions. When we encounter life's profound questions and challenges, our initial response may be to seek quick and immediate solutions from the world around us. We may turn to self-help books, worldly advice, or temporary comforts, hoping they will provide answers to our eternal questions. However, like chasing after mirages, these worldly sources leave us thirsty for true wisdom and understanding.

It is a natural tendency to trust in earthly solutions for the problems that trouble our hearts — worry, stress, and anxiety. Yet, Daniel reminds us that "God gives wisdom to the wise and knowledge to those who have understanding. He reveals deep and secret things" (Daniel 2:21). Placing our trust and hope in anything other than God's wisdom, truth, and comfort is a complete waste of time.

It's a waste of time to trust anything other than God.

In contrast, God's wisdom is an eternal wellspring of knowledge and understanding. His truth provides lasting answers to life's most profound questions. His comfort brings peace that surpasses all understanding. When we turn to Him in our moments of distress, we find a source of solace that will never leave us thirsty or disappointed.

As you encounter life's troubling questions and challenges, learn from King Nebuchadnezzar's example. Embrace the truth that worldly solutions will always fall short of the divine wisdom and comfort that God provides. Seek God's counsel in His Word, turn to Him in prayer, and trust in His unfailing wisdom. In Him, you will find the answers and peace your soul truly seeks, and your trust will never be in vain.

Day 10

A PUZZLING DILEMMA

"With counsel and wisdom Daniel answered Arioch, who had gone out to kill the wise men in Babylon. Also, Daniel went in and asked the King to give him time, that he might tell the king the interpretation."

DANIEL 2:14, 16

LIFE often resembles a complicated puzzle, with numerous pieces that don't seem to fit together. Imagine yourself as an avid puzzle enthusiast, facing a challenging jigsaw puzzle with countless pieces. As you diligently work to assemble the puzzle, you encounter unexpected obstacles — a missing piece, or pieces that appear to belong in multiple places. Frustration may tempt you to force the pieces together, potentially ruining the entire puzzle. However, a patient and discerning puzzler knows that it's crucial to pause, reflect, and seek solutions that bring clarity amidst the complexity.

In Daniel 2, the king's demand had introduced a puzzling challenge into the midst of Babylon. The lives of the wise men, including Daniel and his companions, were in jeopardy, and the pressure to solve the puzzle of the dream was immense. In this critical moment, Daniel exhibited godly patience

*
Often times, moments of crisis do not create character, they reveal it.

and wisdom. This crisis revealed Daniel's character. Instead of hastily attempting to provide a solution, he wisely chose to pause, seeking divine wisdom and inviting his companions — Hananiah, Mishael, and Azariah — to join him in prayer.

Patience in solving a puzzle involves taking the time to study the pieces, recognizing that each one has a unique place in the final picture. Daniel exemplified this by gathering his companions, acknowledging that only God held the key to interpreting the dream and preserving their lives.

Life presents complex puzzles that call for patience and seeking divine guidance. Instead of forcing pieces together in frustration, we can choose to pause and seek clarity. Just as a puzzler may consult a reference image or ask for assistance from others, we can turn to God's Word, seek counsel from trusted friends, and spend time in prayer, asking for His wisdom to bring clarity amidst life's intricate challenges.

Daniel's attitude throughout this challenging situation was one of gratitude and praise for God's faithfulness. When God answered their prayers and revealed the dream's interpretation to Daniel in a night vision, his heart overflowed with thanksgiving. He recognized that only God could provide the missing piece that brought clarity to the complex puzzle.

As you encounter life's intricate puzzles, follow Daniel's example. Embrace distressing dilemmas as opportunities to wait patiently on the Lord, seek His wisdom, and trust in His guidance. Surround yourself with faithful companions who can support you through prayer and encouragement. Let your heart be filled with gratitude and praise for God's incomparable faithfulness as He brings clarity to the complex puzzles of life.

Day 11

PRAYING FRIENDS

"Then Daniel went to his house, and made the decision known to Hananiah, Mishael, and Azariah, his companions, that they might seek mercies from the God of heaven concerning this secret."

DANIEL 2:17-18

IT'S no secret that life often feels like a challenging journey, filled with unexpected twists and turns. Along this path, our choice of companions can make all the difference. In the story of Daniel, we find a profound example of the importance of surrounding ourselves with friends who have a godly influence in our lives.

If you've ever embarked on a treacherous mountain hike, you know that carrying a heavy backpack filled with supplies is exhausting. As you ascend the steep slopes, the weight on your shoulders becomes increasingly burdensome. Traveling this same trail with friends who are willing to share the load makes this trip much more bearable. They offer encouragement, support, and moments of rest, lightening the burden as you journey together.

In Daniel 2, the young prophet faced a daunting task. King Nebuchadnezzar had a mysterious dream, and his decree threatened the lives of all the wise men in Babylon, including Daniel and his friends. In this challenging moment, Daniel didn't face the burden alone. He turned to his faithful companions — Hananiah, Mishael, and Azariah — for support.

Praying friends are one of life's most precious fortunes. Daniel knew this well. He gathered his friends to seek the mercies of the God of heaven through prayer. Together, they shared the weight of the impending crisis, petitioning God for wisdom and guidance. Their unity in prayer was a source of strength, comfort, and encouragement.

Praying friends are one of life's most precious fortunes.

In our own journeys, we encounter various paths and challenges. The friends we choose in life can significantly impact our spiritual walk. It is vital to surround ourselves with friends who share our commitment to God and His ways, friends who uplift us in prayer and provide godly counsel when we face trials and hardships.

However, just as godly friends can be a source of blessing, we must also be cautious about the company we keep. Friends who draw us away from the Lord or encourage us to compromise our faith can lead us down a perilous path. It is crucial to be discerning and prayerful in our choice of companions.

As you reflect on your friendships, consider both the influence you receive and the influence you offer. Be the kind of friend who stands up and kneels by others in prayer. Surround yourself with those who share your commitment to God, and in moments of trial, turn to them for support and encouragement. Together, you can share life's burdens and blessings, finding strength in unity and solace in the presence of praying friends.

Day 12

A THANKFUL HEART

"I thank You and praise You, O God of my fathers; You have given me wisdom and might, and have now made known to me what we asked of You, for You have made known to us the king's demand."

DANIEL 2:23

HAVE you ever been caught in a sudden rainstorm, feeling the cool drops drench you to the bone? Then, just as quickly as it began, the rain subsides, and a brilliant rainbow stretches across the sky. In response to answered prayer, we see Daniel's heart bursting with gratitude and praise, much like the relief and wonder we feel when the rainstorm ends and the rainbow appears.

Daniel faced a life-threatening situation when he and his friends sought God's wisdom to interpret King Nebuchadnezzar's dream. In a time of desperate need, Daniel turned to prayer. Astonishingly, God answered swiftly, revealing the dream's meaning and saving their lives. Daniel's heart overflowed with gratitude and praise.

Yet, we know that life doesn't always follow this quick resolution. There are times when we pray earnestly, and it seems as if God's answers are delayed or hidden. We wait, wondering if God hears our prayers. In those moments, impatience, frustration, and doubt can creep into our hearts, much like the uncertainty that lingers as the storm rumbles on.

However, Daniel's response teaches us that God's faithfulness deserves our gratefulness. It reminds us that God is not only the One who answers our prayers, but also the One who knows the perfect time for each response. Just as the rainstorm eventually yields to the rainbow's beauty, God's timing brings forth His purpose and reveals His goodness.

Thanksgiving and praise are not just appropriate responses to answered prayers; they are expressions of trust in God's unchanging goodness. Gratitude helps us recognize that God's wisdom surpasses our understanding, and His ways are higher than our ways (Isaiah 55:8-9).

> *God's faithfulness deserves our gratefulness.*

Whether you find yourself in a season of immediate answers or waiting on God's timing, let gratitude be the umbrella that shields you from life's downpours. Praise God for His wisdom and sovereignty, knowing that His plans are unfolding according to His divine agenda — trusting that His timing is always best.

In times of answered prayer and in moments of waiting, maintain a heart of thanksgiving. Remember, you can always sing praises even when God seems silent. Trust in the faithfulness of our God, who listens to our prayers and responds in His perfect time. May your life bear witness to the profound truth that God's faithfulness unquestionably deserves our gratefulness, like the rainbow that follows the storm.

Day 13

REFLECTING GOD'S GLORY

"This secret has not been revealed to me because I have more wisdom than anyone living, but for our sakes who make known the interpretation to the king, and that you may know the thoughts of your heart."

DANIEL 2:30

IT'S hard not to be struck with wonder when seeing the beauty of the glowing moon in the vast night sky. It hangs there, radiant and captivating, illuminating the darkness with its soft, silvery glow. But have you ever stopped to think that the moon doesn't have its own light? Instead, it borrows its brilliance from the sun, faithfully reflecting the sun's radiant glory. In many ways, Daniel's approach to revealing King Nebuchadnezzar's dream is similar to the moon's humble reflection of the sun's light.

> Daniel wasn't worried about who got the applause so long as God got the praise.

After much prayer and godly counsel, Daniel acknowledges that the interpretation of the king's dream is not a result of his wisdom or skill but is a divine revelation from God. He wasn't worried about who got the applause, so long as God got the praise. Daniel recognized that he was merely a vessel, a mirror reflecting God's wisdom and power.

Just like the moon shines its borrowed light without seeking recognition, Daniel used his position to highlight the supremacy of God. He didn't seek to elevate himself or bask in the glory of interpreting the dream. Instead, he focused on God's sovereignty and power. In doing so, he reminded King Nebuchadnezzar and all who witnessed this miracle that there is a God in heaven who reveals secrets.

Daniel's humility challenges us today. Often, we seek recognition, applause, and accolades for our accomplishments, even when we are merely instruments in God's hands. Daniel's example calls us to shift our perspective. Our lives are not about us, they are about God and His glory. Just as the moon serves to illuminate the night sky, we are called to shine a spotlight on God's greatness.

God uses us in profound ways, not so that we can get recognition, but so that we can reflect His glory. Our talents, gifts, and opportunities are entrusted to us for His purposes. When we humble ourselves like Daniel and acknowledge that all we have and achieve is through God's grace, we become vessels through which His light can shine brightly in the world.

Let us be inspired by Daniel's humility and commitment to giving God the praise He deserves. As you go about your daily life, remember that you are called to reflect God's glory, just like the moon reflects the sun's light. Seek to shine brightly in a way that draws others closer to God, and let His name be exalted in all you do.

Day 14

AN UNSHAKABLE KINGDOM

"You watched while a stone was cut out without hands, which struck the image on its feet of iron and clay, and broke them in pieces."

DANIEL 2:34

IF you have a garden or lawn, you know how quickly weeds can spring up, only to wither away just as swiftly. These seemingly persistent intruders in our carefully cultivated spaces serve as a poignant metaphor for the transient nature of earthly kingdoms. In Daniel 2:34, we encounter a prophetic vision that vividly illustrates this truth and points us toward a greater, eternal reality.

King Nebuchadnezzar's dream of a colossal statue, with its various segments representing powerful earthly kingdoms throughout history, symbolizes the rise and fall of human empires. It's a reminder that even the mightiest kingdoms, like weeds, have their season, but their dominance eventually fades away.

But hidden within this vision lies a profound and timeless message — an Old Testament reference to Jesus Christ. The "stone cut out without hands" represents Jesus, the heavenly King of kings. In the New Testament, Jesus spoke of Himself as "the stone the builders rejected" becoming the chief cornerstone (Matthew 21:42). Just as this stone shatters the feet of the statue, so does Jesus, the cornerstone, shatter the dominion of earthly kingdoms.

This prophecy reminds us that God is the one who orchestrates the rise and fall of nations. He is the only true King, reigning sovereignly over all of history. While earthly kingdoms may appear formidable and invincible, they are, in reality, fragile and fleeting in the grand scope of God's eternal plan.

As believers, we can take comfort and hope in the fact that the current worldly powers are only temporary. We eagerly await the return of Jesus, who will establish God's eternal kingdom, an unshakable realm where righteousness and peace will reign forever. In a world marked by uncertainty and change, we have an unwavering hope in the unchanging promises of our eternal King.

Jesus is the heavenly King sent to establish the eternal kingdom on earth.

So, as you navigate the challenges and uncertainties of life, remember that the kingdoms of this world, like weeds in a garden, will ultimately fade away. Fix your eyes on the stone, Jesus Christ, who is the cornerstone of God's eternal kingdom. He is the unshakable foundation on which we stand, the One who will bring about the fulfillment of God's glorious plan. May this truth fill your heart with hope and confidence as you await the triumphant return of our King.

Day 15

DISAPPOINTING IDOLS

"Nebuchadnezzar the king made an image of gold, whose height was sixty cubits and its width six cubits. He set it up in the plain of Dura in Babylon."

DANIEL 3:1

HAVE you ever met someone you've admired from afar for a long time, only to discover that they weren't who you thought they were? The disappointment in such moments can be profound, leaving us with a sense of emptiness and disillusionment. In Daniel 3:1, we see a story of a golden idol erected in the province of Babylon, but beyond the physical image, it serves as a powerful metaphor for the idols we often build in our own lives.

An idol is anything that diverts our attention and worship away from God.

Idols can take many forms — not just statues of gold or silver. They can be relationships, material possessions, career ambitions, or even our own self-image. We sometimes place these idols on a pedestal, expecting them to fulfill us, bring us happiness, or provide the security we crave. But like the golden image in Babylon, these idols often let us down in the end.

Consider the disappointment of meeting someone you've idolized for years, only to realize that they are flawed, just like everyone else. The danger of setting up idols in our lives is that they divert our attention and worship away from God, the only One who is truly worthy of our devotion.

When we place our hopes and dreams in something or someone other than God, we set ourselves up for disappointment. It's not that these things are inherently bad, but when they become the center of our attention and affection, they take the place that belongs to God alone.

The Bible warns us against this in Exodus 20:3-5: "You shall have no other gods before Me. You shall not make for yourself a carved image—any likeness of anything that is in heaven above, or that is in the earth beneath, or that is in the water under the earth; you shall not bow down to them nor serve them. For I, the Lord your God, am a jealous God."

The story of the golden idol teaches us that idols, whether physical or of the heart, will eventually disappoint and fail us. But God never disappoints. He is constant, faithful, and unchanging. When we place Him at the center of our lives, we find lasting fulfillment and purpose.

So, let us examine our hearts today. Are there idols we've set up that steal our attention and worship away from God? Are there people or things we've idolized, expecting them to fulfill us in ways only God can? Let's remember that our Creator, the One who formed us and knows us intimately, is the only One truly deserving of our devotion. May we turn away from the idols of our hearts and turn toward Him. In doing so, we will find the fulfillment and purpose we seek, and our hearts will be filled with the true joy that comes from a genuine relationship with the living God.

Day 16

COURAGEOUS FAITH

"Therefore at that time certain Chaldeans came forward and accused the Jews."

DANIEL 3:8

IN the world of law enforcement, solving a complex crime often depends on gathering clues and evidence that point to the truth. Detectives meticulously examine each piece of information, searching for the key that will unlock the mystery. Just as in a police investigation, the actions of Shadrach, Meshach, and Abednego in Daniel 3 provide us with clear evidence of their courageous faith and trust in God.

These three men found themselves in a perilous situation. King Nebuchadnezzar had erected a golden image and commanded all to bow down and worship it. But Shadrach, Meshach, and Abednego knew that such an act would violate their deeply held faith in the one true God. So, when the music played and everyone else bowed, they remained standing tall. Their brave stance was like a beacon of light in the darkest of times.

In the face of fear, these three friends demonstrated a faith that allowed them to stand up when it was safer to lie low. They understood the pressure to conform to the world's demands, and they knew the consequences of disobedience could be deadly. Yet, they refused to compromise their faith, even in the shadow of the fiery furnace.

In our own lives, we too face pressures to conform to the values and norms of this world. These pressures can be so intense that we may be tempted to give in, fearing the consequences or what others might think. But faith, as exemplified by Shadrach, Meshach, and Abednego, provides us with the strength to stand firm.

Faith allows you to stand up when it's safer to lie low.

Consider this: What evidence in your life points to your faith in God? Just as detectives follow the trail of clues to uncover the truth, others may look at our actions to discern the authenticity of our faith. Do our choices, our words, and our deeds testify to our trust in God, even when it's difficult?

The story of Shadrach, Meshach, and Abednego challenges us to be courageous in our faith, especially when the world pressures us to conform. Our willingness to stand up for what we believe in, even when it's risky, becomes a powerful testimony to the strength of our relationship with God.

Today, pause to reflect on your life and ask yourself if you are standing firm in the face of accusations or opposition to your Christian beliefs. Let your faith be the evidence that cannot be denied, just as the courageous actions of these three men were undeniable in the court of King Nebuchadnezzar. Remember, faith allows you to stand up when it's safer to lie low, and in doing so, you shine as a light in the darkness, pointing others toward the truth of God's love and grace.

Day 17

GOD'S MYSTERIOUS WAYS

"Our God whom we serve is able to deliver us from the burning fiery furnace. But if not, let it be known, we do not serve your gods, nor worship the gold image."

DANIEL 3:17-18

AT the center of every thrilling novel, we find ourselves immersed in suspense, eagerly turning each page, seeking resolution to the mystery that unfolds. As the anticipation builds, we are held captive, excited to see how the story will conclude. Shadrach, Meshach, and Abednego's remarkable faith in the face of a fiery trial mirrors the suspense of such a tale. These men faced a test of faith that held the entire kingdom in suspense and teach us that full submission to God surrenders the final scenario to Him.

Shadrach, Meshach, and Abednego exhibited a profound trust and dependency on God that went beyond their personal desires and aspirations. In the face of an intimidating statue and a fiery furnace that threatened to consume them, they refused to bow to the pressure of the crowd or the threats of the powerful king. Instead, they chose to submit their lives fully to the sovereign God, placing their trust in His wisdom and plan.

In the midst of this intense trial, these men displayed immense trust in God. Their confident words echo with resounding faith. They believed that God had the power to rescue them from the impending danger, just as we often hope for the best outcomes in the suspenseful narratives of our own lives.

However, what sets Shadrach, Meshach, and Abednego apart is their willing submission to God, as expressed in the phrase, "But if not..." In these three simple words, we find the essence of their confidence and faith. They were willing to trust God with the final outcome, even if it meant enduring the fiery trial. Their faith was anchored not in a specific outcome, but in the character and power of the Almighty.

Full submission to God surrenders the final scenario to Him.

In life, we too face countless trials and uncertainties. We may pray for specific outcomes, just as Shadrach, Meshach, and Abednego hoped to be delivered from the furnace. Yet, like them, we must recognize that God's ways are above our ways. He is the author of our story, and His plot lines often take unexpected turns. But our trust in Him can remain unshaken because we know that He is capable of writing something greater.

The story of these brave young men teaches us that we can be content in the midst of uncertainty. We can have assurance that God is working out His perfect plan, even if it doesn't align with our desires. Submission to His will allows us to trust the One who is writing our story through every suspenseful twist and mysterious turn as it unfolds in our lives.

Just as a thrilling novel keeps us engaged until the very end, so too can our trust in God keep us steadfast in the midst of life's uncertainties. As we surrender to His will, we can rest assured that He is the master storyteller, crafting a narrative that will ultimately bring glory to His name and fulfillment to our souls. So let us trust Him, even when the plot thickens, knowing that in His hands, our story will always end in triumph.

Day 18

CONTROLLING OUR TEMPER

"Then Nebuchadnezzar was full of fury, and the expression on his face changed. He spoke and commanded that they heat the furnace seven times more than it was usually heated."

DANIEL 3:19

LIFE has a way of cranking down on us, just like a jack-in-the-box, waiting for that perfect moment to spring forth when we least expect it. Anger, much like the surprise inside the jack-in-the-box, can pop out of us when things don't go our way or when we feel the pressures of life bearing down on us. This seemingly harmless toy, coiled with tension beneath its cheerful exterior is a perfect metaphor for anger. In the Book of Daniel, we encounter a king who could conquer nations but couldn't control his emotions.

Controlling our temper is a great achievement when life cranks up the tension.

Nebuchadnezzar, a powerful ruler, was accustomed to having his every whim obeyed. When Shadrach, Meshach, and Abed-Nego refused to bow down to his golden image, his anger flared like a jack-in-the-box suddenly released. The king's fury was uncontrollable, and he ordered the furnace to be heated seven times hotter than usual. His anger knew no bounds, and he was willing to make an example out of these three faithful young men.

How often do we find ourselves in situations where our emotions, particularly anger, threaten to burst forth like that jack-in-the-box? Just as you turn the crank, life often cranks down on us with stress, disappointment, and unmet expectations. When the pressure builds, the lid of anger can pop open without warning. However, the Bible warns us in Proverbs 16:32 that "he who is slow to anger is better than the mighty, and he who rules his spirit than he who takes a city." It reminds us that controlling our temper is a greater achievement than conquering nations.

James 1:19 also admonishes us, "So then, my beloved brethren, let every man be swift to hear, slow to speak, slow to wrath." This verse reminds us to be careful with our words and to be patient in the face of frustration. The Bible also warns us that the wrath of man does not produce the righteousness of God, and when anger takes control, it often leads to regret.

Imagine if Shadrach, Meshach, and Abed-Nego had responded to the king's command with anger and defiance. They could have easily lost their lives in a fit of rage. Instead, they chose to remain steadfast in their faith, trusting in God's deliverance.

So, as we reflect on the story of Nebuchadnezzar and his fierce fury, let us challenge ourselves to extinguish anger quickly before it has the chance to unexpectedly pop out and frighten everyone around us. Let us strive to be slow to anger and quick to forgive, emulating the righteousness of God. Just like those faithful young men, our steadfastness in the face of anger can be a powerful testimony to our faith in the Lord.

Day 19

BUILDING FAITH MUSCLES

"And he commanded certain mighty men of valor who were to bind Shadrach, Meshach, and Abed-Nego, and cast them into the burning fiery furnace."

DANIEL 3:20

WHEN it comes to physical fitness, there's a saying that goes, "No pain, no gain." This principle is deeply rooted in the idea that in order to build strong muscles and increase stamina, one must endure discomfort and even pain through weightlifting and strenuous workouts. Similarly, in our spiritual journey, we encounter trials and tribulations that may seem uncomfortable and painful. However, just as lifting weights leads to stronger muscles, God uses trials to refine and strengthen our faith.

The Bible reminds us that the testing of our faith is often tried by fire. In Daniel 3:20, we see Shadrach, Meshach, and Abed-Nego cast into a fiery furnace for their faith in God. This dramatic event serves as a powerful illustration of the trials we face as believers. Being a follower of Jesus does not make us immune to trials and tribulations. In fact, these trials can be a means by which our faith is tested and strengthened.

James 1:2-4 tells us, "Count it all joy when you fall into various trials, knowing that the testing of your faith produces patience. But let patience have its perfect work, that you may be perfect and complete, lacking nothing." Just as lifting weights builds physical endurance, enduring trials in faith produces perseverance and godly character in us. It is through these difficult times that we grow closer to God and become more like Christ.

In John 16:33, Jesus encourages us with these words: "In this world you will have tribulation, but be of good cheer, I have overcome the world." Jesus acknowledges the challenges we will face as believers, but assures us that He has already conquered the world. In fact, in lifting the cross, Jesus endured suffering not so that we don't have to, but so that we know how to. Just as a weightlifter needs a spotter to assist them when lifting heavy weights, Jesus is right there with us, providing the support we need to endure trials and emerge stronger in our faith.

In lifting the cross, Jesus endured suffering not so that we don't have to but so that we know how to.

As we face trials, it's essential to have God's perspective. Instead of seeing them as obstacles, view them as opportunities for spiritual growth. Remember that God is using these challenges to shape you into the person He created you to be. Just as a weightlifter visualizes themselves getting stronger with each repetition, envision yourself growing stronger in the Lord through every trial.

Trials are like spiritual weightlifting; they can be uncomfortable and painful, but they are essential for building our faith muscles and stamina. Just as lifting weights leads to physical strength, enduring trials leads to spiritual strength, perseverance, and godly character. Keep in mind that Jesus is your faithful spotter, providing the support you need in times of trouble. So, when you face trials embrace them with joy, knowing that through them your faith is growing stronger, and you are becoming more like Christ.

Day 20

GOD'S SOOTHING PROTECTION

"He answered, 'Look! I see four men loose, walking in the midst of the fire; and they are not hurt, and the form of the fourth is like the Son of God.'"

DANIEL 3:25

IMAGINE being out in the scorching sun without protection. You would soon feel the burning effect on your skin, causing discomfort and pain. Just as we apply aloe vera gel to soothe our physical soreness, we often find ourselves in fiery trials that leave us spiritually burned. In these moments, we can draw inspiration from the story of Shadrach, Meshach, and Abed-Nego in the fiery furnace and the comforting promise of Jesus' presence.

In Daniel 3:25, we see a remarkable sight: Shadrach, Meshach, and Abed-Nego, who were cast into the fiery furnace for refusing to bow down to a golden image, were not alone. There, in the midst of the flames, they encountered the fourth person — the Son of God. In the midst of their trial, Jesus was with them, protecting them from the harm of the fire.

Just as Shadrach, Meshach, and Abed-Nego faced their fiery trial, we too encounter challenges, difficulties, and tribulations in our lives. These trials can be like the relentless rays of the sun, scorching our souls and causing emotional and spiritual discomfort. But take heart, for Jesus promises His presence in every painful furnace.

When we experience trials, it's easy to feel alone and overwhelmed. But remember, you are never alone. Jesus draws near to the brokenhearted and inclines His ear to our desperate prayers (Psalm 34:18). His presence is like the soothing touch of aloe vera gel on our sunburned souls. It brings relief, comfort, and healing to our wounded and weary spirits.

Jesus promises His presence in every painful furnace.

No matter how hot the fire of trials become, Jesus is there to protect you. His love is the ultimate SPF (Spiritual Protection Factor) that shields you from the burning effects of life's challenges. His grace cools the flames of anxiety, fear, and doubt. His presence provides the shade you need to find rest and restoration from the relentless rays of pain.

In the midst of life's fiery trials, remember Daniel 3:25: "Look! I see four men loose, walking in the midst of the fire; and they are not hurt, and the form of the fourth is like the Son of God." Just as Jesus stood with Shadrach, Meshach, and Abed-Nego in the furnace, He stands with you in your trials today, even in the most intense circumstances.

So, apply the soothing balm of His presence to your wounds, knowing that Jesus is the ultimate SPF that protects you from the harmful burning effects of life's challenges. He is the Son of God, the One who promises to never leave you nor forsake you. With Jesus by your side, you can face any trial, knowing that you are never alone, and that His love will always be your ultimate protection in every painful trial of life.

Day 21

A CREDIBLE WITNESS

"Nebuchadnezzar spoke, saying, 'Blessed be the God of Shadrach, Meshach, and Abed-Nego, who sent His Angel and delivered His servants who trusted in Him, they have yielded their bodies, that they should not serve nor worship any god except their own God!'"

DANIEL 3:28

IN the solemn chamber of a courtroom, a witness steps forward to bear testimony, to share their account of what they have seen and experienced. Their credibility is paramount, for their words can sway the minds of the jury, shaping the course of justice. In the same way, the story of Shadrach, Meshach, and Abed-Nego in Daniel 3:28 serves as a powerful testimony — a credible witness — of God's deliverance.

Seeing God's work in our lives is an effective witness to others.

Imagine these three men standing in the metaphorical witness stand of life, facing the fiery furnace, not knowing if they would survive. Their unquestionable faith in the One true God led them to declare, "Our God whom we serve is able to deliver us from the burning fiery furnace, and He will deliver us from your hand, O king" (Daniel 3:17). Their words echoed with conviction, demonstrating their trust in God's sovereignty.

As the story unfolds, their trust was not in vain. God intervened in a miraculous way, rescuing them from the furnace's flames. King Nebuchadnezzar himself declared the power of God, recognizing that they had defied his command and emerged unscathed. In the courtroom of Nebuchadnezzar's palace, Shadrach, Meshach, and Abed-Nego were credible witnesses to God's saving grace and power.

Their testimony reminds us that our faith, especially during times of adversity, can be the most compelling testimony we offer to the world. Seeing God at work in our lives is an effective witness to others. We may share the gospel with eloquent words, but it is our authentic expression of faith lived out in the moments of suffering and pain that often draws people to God.

Consider the impact your faith can have on those around you, especially those who doubt God. When we face life's fiery trials with complete trust in God, our lives become a living testament to His faithfulness. People may not always be convinced by our words, but they can be deeply moved by the genuine faith we display in the midst of life's challenges. Never underestimate the impact your faith can have on a suspicious seeker of truth, for your life can become indisputable evidence pointing to the greatness of our God.

As you walk through the various seasons of life, remember that your trust in God, especially in times of trial, can serve as a powerful testimony to those around you. Just like credible witnesses in a courtroom, your life can bear witness to God's faithfulness and deliverance. Let your faith shine brightly, for in doing so, you may lead others to discover the profound truth of God's love and saving grace.

Day 22

DECLARING GOD'S GOODNESS

> "I thought it good to declare the signs and wonders that the Most High God has worked for me. How great are His signs, and how mighty His wonders! His kingdom is an everlasting kingdom, and His dominion is from generation to generation."
>
> **DANIEL 4:2-3**

HAVE you ever been on an airplane during a storm? The experience can be quite unnerving. The turbulence shakes the plane, rain pelts against the windows, and darkness surrounds you. It's as if you're caught in the midst of a tempest, with no way out. But then, something amazing happens. The plane begins to ascend, rising above the stormy clouds.

Below the clouds, it's rainy, dark, and turbulent — much like the difficult circumstances we face in life. We may find ourselves struggling with problems, worries, and uncertainties. It's easy to get lost in the chaos, focusing solely on the storm that rages beneath us.

But just as the airplane ascends above the clouds, we too can rise above our troubles. Daniel 4:2-3 reminds us of the importance of declaring God's goodness and mighty works in our lives. When we do this, we shift our focus from the stormy circumstances below to the One who reigns supreme above it all.

In the darkest of times, we must remember to declare God's goodness and the mighty works He has performed in our lives. These acts of praise and thanksgiving become our ascent above the clouds of adversity. They help us rise to a place of peace and serenity, where we can see God's sovereignty and grace more clearly.

As you reflect on your life, consider all the mighty works of God. Remember the times when He provided, healed, comforted, and guided you. Think about the moments when His presence was tangible, and His love was undeniable. These are the signs and wonders that King Nebuchadnezzar learned in his trial — evidence of God's greatness and faithfulness.

Praising God becomes our ascent above the stormy clouds of adversity.

No matter how turbulent the storms of life may be, God's kingdom remains everlasting, and His dominion spans generations. He is above it all, and His goodness shines like the sun beyond the grey skies and stormy clouds. Hold on to His promises, trust in His sovereignty, and declare His mighty works.

Today, take time to declare God's goodness and wondrous works in your life. Lift your focus from the storms that surround you, and fix your eyes on the One who is above it all. In doing so, you will find peace, strength, and a renewed sense of awe for the Most High God, whose love and power endures forever.

Day 23

SATURATED IN THE HOLY SPIRIT

> "But at last Daniel came before me (his name is Belteshazzar, according to the name of my god; in him is the Spirit of the Holy God), and I told the dream before him."
>
> **DANIEL 4:8**

IMAGINE a chef preparing a sumptuous meal, marinating a piece of meat with a blend of spices and sauces, allowing the flavors to infuse every fiber. The result is a tender, juicy, and flavorful dish that delights the senses. In a similar way, the Holy Spirit tenderizes and saturates our lives with His presence, infusing the fruit of the Spirit into our character.

In Daniel 4:8, we catch a glimpse of Daniel, a man in whom "is the Spirit of the Holy God." Daniel's life was marinated and saturated with the Holy Spirit, just like that perfectly prepared piece of meat. As he stood before King Nebuchadnezzar, his life testified to the transformative power of the Spirit dwelling within him.

The process of marinating and tenderizing meat requires time and intentionality. Similarly, our journey of being saturated in the Holy Spirit is a lifelong pursuit. When we allow the Spirit to work in us, we become spiritually tenderized, enabling us to respond to life's challenges with grace and love.

Think about a beautifully cooked steak. When you cut into it, the exquisite flavors punctuate every bite. Likewise, when we are filled with the Holy Spirit and walking in step with Him, more love, joy, peace, patience, kindness, goodness, faithfulness, gentleness, and self-control ooze out when life cuts deep. Others can taste and see the difference in our character.

The Holy Spirit is not merely a force or an influence; He is our Comforter and Counselor. Just as a well-marinated piece of meat is flavorful to the core, the Holy Spirit works deep within us, comforting us in times of distress and guiding us along life's unpredictable paths.

As believers, we are called to spend time saturating our hearts and minds with the Holy Spirit. Like marinating meat, we must soak ourselves in God's Word, meditating on His promises and emptying ourselves of worldly desires. It's through this surrender that we experience true change, and the more we become conduits for the Holy Spirit's work.

May we be those whose lives are tenderized by the Holy Spirit, marinating in His presence, and flavored with the character of Christ.

In a world that hungers for authenticity and goodness, may we be those whose lives are tenderized by the Holy Spirit, marinating in His presence, and flavored with the character of Christ. As we yield to His guidance and work, we become vessels through which the world can taste and see that the Lord is good (Psalm 34:8). Just as the finest marinated meat is a testament to the skill of the chef, our lives, infused with the Holy Spirit, become a testament to the transformative power of God's grace.

Day 24

GOD'S PRUNING PURPOSE

"Nevertheless leave the stump and roots in the earth, bound with a band of iron and bronze, in the tender grass of the field. Let it be wet with the dew of heaven, and let him graze with the beasts on the earth."

DANIEL 4:15

IN the world of horticulture, there is a practice known as pruning. It involves carefully cutting away certain branches and leaves from fruit trees to ensure they grow healthier, bear more fruit, and live longer. The skilled orchard horticulturalist understands that sometimes badly diseased or unproductive branches must be cut off to promote the overall vitality of the tree. This process can seem harsh, but it is vital for the tree's long-term health and productivity.

God's correction is never intended to destroy us, but to change us.

In Daniel 4, we encounter a powerful analogy of pruning and restoration in the life of King Nebuchadnezzar. The king, filled with pride and arrogance, faced the judgment of God. Just as a diseased tree must be pruned, God chose to humble Nebuchadnezzar by removing him as the ruler of Babylon. But even in this judgment, there was a glimmer of hope. God, like a wise orchard horticulturalist, left the stump and roots intact.

This story reminds us that God's correction is never intended to destroy us, but to change us. Just as a pruned tree can grow back healthier and produce more abundant fruit, God's discipline is meant to remove the dead and diseased aspects of our lives so that we can become spiritually healthy and bear godly fruit.

The stump and roots left in the ground in Nebuchadnezzar's case symbolize hope. Despite the drastic measures taken, God didn't abandon him. He provided the potential for restoration and growth. This act of divine pruning was not only about correction, but also about redemption. Nebuchadnezzar's heart was not beyond God's reach, and in due time, he acknowledged the sovereignty of the true God and was restored to his kingdom (Daniel 4:34-37).

In our own lives, God often prunes and cuts off things that hinder our spiritual growth and bear no godly fruit. It might be painful and humbling, but it's always an act of love. God desires to see us flourish, and sometimes that means removing the pride, selfishness, or sinful habits that hinder our relationship with Him.

Just like Nebuchadnezzar's fall led to his eventual restoration, God can take the greatest of falls and failures in our lives to produce the best spiritual fruit and new life. When we place ourselves in God's loving and caring hands, we can trust that His pruning is for our good. It is a process of transformation, renewal, and second chances.

So, remember when God prunes and cuts away things in your life, it's a sign of His love and desire to see you flourish. Just like the orchard horticulturalist tends to the trees for a bountiful harvest, God tends to your heart for the abundant life He has planned for you. Trust in His wisdom, embrace His correction, and find hope in His promise of restoration.

Day 25
THE DISEASE OF SIN

"Therefore, O king, let my advice be acceptable to you; break off your sins by being righteous, and your iniquities by showing mercy to the poor."

DANIEL 4:27

IN our modern world, we have come to appreciate the importance of regular check-ups and cutting-edge medical technology in maintaining our physical health. These check-ups allow us to detect early signs of sickness and disease, enabling us to receive timely treatment and prevent further complications. Just as we value our physical well-being, it is equally crucial to recognize the state of our spiritual health.

In the book of Daniel, we find an intriguing analogy of spiritual health in the advice given to King Nebuchadnezzar. Daniel, a faithful servant of God, warned the king about a disease far more deadly than any physical ailment — the disease of sin. He implored the king to heed his advice, "break off your sins by being righteous, and your iniquities by showing mercy to the poor."

Consider for a moment the urgency with which doctors recommend addressing an illness detected in its early stages. They understand that a delay in treatment can lead to more significant problems. Similarly, Daniel's counsel emphasizes the need for King Nebuchadnezzar to act swiftly and decisively in dealing with the disease of sin. He essentially tells the king, "Don't allow stubborn reluctance to keep you from a speedy repentance."

In our own lives, sin can silently infiltrate our hearts and minds, leading to spiritual decay and separation from God. Just as modern medicine relies on early detection, we must be vigilant in recognizing the signs of sin within us. The symptoms may vary — pride, greed, anger, lust, or any other transgression against God's commandments. Whatever form it takes, sin must be addressed promptly.

Don't allow stubborn reluctance to keep you from a speedy repentance.

Even Jesus Himself challenged His disciples to go to extreme measures to "cut off" sin in their lives. In Matthew 5:30, He said, "And if your right hand causes you to sin, cut it off and cast it from you; for it is more profitable for you that one of your members perish than for your whole body to be cast into hell."

But the good news is that God is not only the Great Physician but also a loving and merciful Father. When we confess our sins and turn to Him in repentance, He is faithful and just to forgive us and cleanse us from all unrighteousness (1 John 1:9). Just as a patient trusts their doctor's expertise, we must trust God's advice for the healing of our souls through the forgiveness of sin.

As we strive to maintain our physical health through regular check-ups and early intervention, let us also be diligent in evaluating our spiritual health. Don't allow the disease of sin to fester and grow. Take God's advice as the ultimate remedy, and with a repentant heart, break off your sins, and find healing and restoration in His boundless grace and mercy.

Day 26

THE PROBLEM WITH PROCRASTINATION

> "All this came upon King Nebuchadnezzar. At the end of the twelve months as he was walking about the royal palace of Babylon."
>
> **DANIEL 4:28-29**

IT'S never wise to neglect a problem, hoping it would simply go away on its own. Much like ignoring a leaky roof that can lead to rotting wood, mold growth, and even structural damage to your home, neglecting sin in our lives can lead to devastating consequences.

In the book of Daniel, we encounter the story of King Nebuchadnezzar, a powerful and prideful ruler of Babylon. God, in His mercy, gave Nebuchadnezzar a warning about his pride and arrogance. He provided the king with a whole year to reflect and change his ways. However, instead of addressing his sin promptly, Nebuchadnezzar put it off, thinking he could deal with it later. Little did he know that delaying his repentance would lead to dire consequences.

Don't wait until later to get right what God is warning you about now.

The moment Nebuchadnezzar boasted about his great achievements, God's judgment swiftly fell upon him. His kingdom was taken away, and he was driven into the wilderness, where he lived like a wild animal for seven years. It was only through this humbling experience that Nebuchadnezzar came to recognize the sovereignty of the Most High God.

This story serves as a powerful reminder for us today. When God convicts us of sin or points out areas in our lives that need correction, we must not delay or ignore His warning. Just as a leaky roof requires immediate attention before it causes more significant damage, so too does sin in our lives demand prompt repentance.

The lesson is clear: Don't put off until later to get right what God is warning you about now. The longer we wait, the more deeply rooted sin can become, leading to spiritual rot, bitterness, and distance from God. Just as Nebuchadnezzar suffered the consequences of his pride, we too can experience the consequences of unaddressed sin.

Let us follow Nebuchadnezzar's example in his eventual humility. Instead of delaying, let us take our concerns to God immediately. Ask Him to inspect our hearts for cracks and leaks that have the potential to undermine our relationship with Him. When God reveals these areas to us, let us seek His forgiveness, His cleansing, and His transformation in our lives.

In doing so, we can ensure that our spiritual foundation remains secure and strong, standing firmly on the solid rock of God's grace and love. Don't delay, turn to God today and experience the freedom and restoration that comes from addressing sin promptly.

Day 27

THE PERILS OF PRIDE

"The king spoke, saying, 'Is not this great Babylon, that I have built for a royal dwelling by my mighty power and for the honor of my majesty?' While the word was still in the king's mouth, a voice fell from heaven: 'King Nebuchadnezzar: the kingdom has departed from you!'"

DANIEL 4:30-31

IN the heart of the Cleveland National Forest, a seemingly insignificant creature, the Gold-Spotted Oak Borer beetle, quietly wreaks havoc on the majestic coastal live oak trees that have stood for centuries. These mighty oaks, with their towering branches and deep-rooted strength, appear invincible. Yet, this tiny insect, smaller than a grain of rice, possesses the potential to bring these giants to their early demise.

Much like these formidable trees, we often find ourselves soaring to great heights in our lives. However, if we're not vigilant, success can often produce an excess of pride, blinding us to the dangers lurking within. The story of King Nebuchadnezzar serves as a vivid reminder of the perils of pride.

Nebuchadnezzar, the once great king of Babylon, stood atop the pinnacle of his achievements. In Daniel 4:30, he exclaimed, "Is not this great Babylon, that I have built for a royal dwelling by my mighty power and for the honor of my majesty?" His pride knew no bounds as he attributed his accomplishments solely to his own strength and wisdom.

But just as the Gold-Spotted Oak Borer beetle bores its way through the bark of a majestic oak, so too did pride begin to eat away at Nebuchadnezzar's soul. In an instant, God's voice thundered from heaven, pronouncing judgment on the haughty king. The kingdom was stripped away, and Nebuchadnezzar was driven from the society he had once ruled.

The Bible warns us repeatedly against the dangers of pride. Proverbs 3:34 tells us that "God resists the proud but gives grace to the humble." Like the relentless beetle gnawing at the core of the oak, pride can slowly consume our lives, separating us from God's grace and favor.

Even the smallest of pride can destroy the greatest of people.

Proverbs 16:18 also reminds us, "Pride goes before destruction, and a haughty spirit before a fall." Just as the coastal live oak trees, with all their strength and grandeur, succumb to the tiny beetle, a fall is imminent when pride is rampant in our hearts.

In the same way that the Gold-Spotted Oak Borer beetle threatens mighty oaks, the smallest seeds of pride can destroy the greatest of people. Guard your heart against the insidious invasion of pride, lest it bore its way into your life and destroy you from the inside out. May we humbly acknowledge that all we have and all we are is by the grace of God. In our humility, we find strength, and in our dependence on Him, we stand tall and unshaken, like the mighty oaks, not in our own might, but in the grace of our Creator.

Day 28

THE LIGHT IN A DIAMOND

"I, Nebuchadnezzar, lifted my eyes to heaven, and my understanding returned to me; and I blessed the Most High and praised Him who lives forever."

DANIEL 4:34

IMAGINE a skilled jeweler delicately holding a rough diamond, poised to transform it into a dazzling masterpiece. Before this gem can shine with its full brilliance, it must undergo a meticulous process. The jeweler carefully inspects it under the unforgiving glare of a powerful light, searching for any imperfections or blemishes hidden within its depths. Through this process, the diamond is refined until it radiates with a flawless beauty.

Similarly, our lives are like rough diamonds in the hands of our Heavenly Jeweler, God Himself. Just as the jeweler uses light and microscopes to peer deep into precious gems, so does God use the trials of life and the light of His Word to reveal our hidden blemishes. In Daniel 4:34, we find King Nebuchadnezzar's remarkable transformation from arrogance to humility, and his story provides profound insights into this divine process.

Nebuchadnezzar, once a prideful and self-reliant king, was humbled by God's sovereign hand. He was brought to his knees and driven into the wilderness of madness, much like the Israelites who wandered in the desert for forty years. God allowed this trial to humble and test them, to see what was in their hearts, and whether they would obey His Word (Deuteronomy 8:2).

In the midst of his trials and tribulations, Nebuchadnezzar finally lifted his eyes to heaven. It was only then that his understanding returned, and he saw God for who He truly is — the Most High who reigns forever. The closer we get to God, the clearer we see our sin, just as the jeweler's light exposes the flaws of the diamond.

When Nebuchadnezzar humbled himself and acknowledged God's sovereignty, he responded with submission and worship. He recognized that God's dominion is everlasting, and His kingdom endures from generation to generation. His transformation was a testament to the power of humility and God's redemptive grace.

> *The closer we get to God, the clearer we see our sin.*

Likewise, when we face trials and difficulties, we must lift our eyes upon Jesus. Allow God to expose and correct any character flaws within us. Embrace humility, for it is in these moments of brokenness that we can truly see God and our desperate need for Him. Just as the jeweler's light reveals the hidden imperfections within the diamond, so God's light and truth illuminate our hearts, showing us the way to become more like Him.

Today, let us be willing to embrace the refining process, allowing God to shine His light into the recesses of our souls. As we do, may we, like Nebuchadnezzar, lift our voices in worship and praise to the Most High, acknowledging His everlasting dominion and surrendering our lives to His glorious and transformative grace.

Day 29
WARNING SIGNS

"Belshazzar the king made a great feast for a thousand of his lords, and drank wine in their presence."

DANIEL 5:1

Drive down any road and eventually you'll come across various signs: some giving directions, others providing crucial information, and still others warning of hazards or danger ahead. These signs are there to guide and protect you. Ignoring them can lead to severe consequences, just as King Belshazzar's disregard had dire consequences for him.

In Daniel 5:1, we find King Belshazzar of Babylon throwing a grand feast for a thousand of his nobles. While the wine flowed and the music played, he ignored the signs of impending danger. The advancing Persian army, led by Cyrus, was at his doorstep, ready to invade. It's as if Belshazzar had chosen to party in the middle of a war zone, blissfully ignorant of the impending peril in front of him.

It's a misstep to ignore the enemy at the doorstep.

This scenario can be likened to our lives as well. We often find ourselves distracted by worldly pleasures, celebrations, and indulgences, oblivious to the spiritual threats that lurk around us. King Belshazzar's drunken celebration mirrors the times when we let our guards down and allow ourselves to be consumed by the cares of this world, forgetting that there's a spiritual battle raging around us.

Belshazzar's situation is a chilling reminder that ignoring the enemy at the doorstep can lead to dire consequences. In our spiritual journey, we too often face threats, both from the outside and within. The Bible warns us that Satan is like a roaring lion, seeking whom he may devour (1 Peter 5:8). Sin also crouches at our door, waiting for the opportunity to pounce and destroy us (Genesis 4:7).

Just as King Belshazzar foolishly ignored the signs of the approaching Persian army, we must not disregard the spiritual threats that surround us. This story teaches us that it's a misstep to ignore the enemy at the doorstep. We need to be vigilant, watchful, and discerning. We must heed God's warning signs and stay close to Him, seeking His guidance and protection.

Take a moment to reflect on your life. Have you, like Belshazzar, ever ignored the signs of impending spiritual danger? Have you become complacent in your faith, relying on your own strength and security? It's time to wake up and pay attention to the spiritual sirens and road signs that God provides.

Let us commit to being more attentive and vigilant in our walk with God. May we heed His wake-up calls and take His warnings seriously. Just as we wouldn't drive past road signs without considering their significance, let us not disregard God's guidance and protection in our lives. In doing so, we can navigate the spiritual journey ahead with wisdom and discernment, avoiding the traps that lie in wait, and ultimately find our true security in Him.

Day 30
WRITING ON THE WALL

"In the same hour the fingers of a man's hand appeared and wrote on the wall of the king's palace; and the king saw the part of the hand that wrote."

DANIEL 5:5

THE phrase "The writing is on the wall" has become a common idiom in our culture, signifying a symbol of pending doom or destruction. This saying is derived from a biblical account found in the book of Daniel, in which God's shocking and unexpected intervention grabbed the attention of a prideful king and announced punishment for his offensive actions toward God. In Daniel 5:5, we find an extraordinary display of God's power, which serves as a profound lesson on how God uses wake-up calls to prevent great downward falls.

God's wake-up calls prevent great downward falls.

Belshazzar, the king of Babylon, was living a life marked by arrogance and disregard for God. His actions and choices were offensive to the Almighty, but he seemed oblivious to the impending consequences. However, in a single, dramatic moment, God's divine intervention shattered the king's false sense of security. The fingers of a man's hand appeared and wrote a message on the palace wall, leaving the king in awe and trembling. This supernatural occurrence was a wake-up call of the most extraordinary kind.

Similarly, God often uses various means to get our attention when we stray from His ways. These wake-up calls are not meant to bring destruction but to evoke conviction and change in our lives. Just as Belshazzar's pride led to his downfall, our pride and disobedience can also lead us into situations of spiritual peril. God's wake-up calls are intended to guide us back to the right path and protect us from hurt and harm.

While God may not always write on a wall to grab our attention, He has indeed written His Word to guide and mature us. The Bible contains the timeless wisdom and truths that are meant to direct our steps and provide insight into God's heart. His Word serves as a lamp to our feet and a light to our path (Psalm 119:105). As we read and meditate on the Scriptures, we discover the will of God and gain a deeper understanding of His character and desires for our lives.

Belshazzar's story teaches us the importance of paying attention to God's wake-up calls. It's not a matter of if we will receive them, but when. These calls may come in the form of conviction in our hearts, wise counsel from others, challenging circumstances, or moments of divine intervention. They are opportunities for us to acknowledge our wrongdoings and seek God's forgiveness and guidance.

God's corrections are not meant to harm us, but to steer us in the right direction. They are His loving way of preventing us from making choices that could lead to our downfall. So, let us be vigilant, humble, and receptive to God's wake-up calls, whether they are as dramatic as a writing on the wall or as subtle as a gentle whisper in our hearts. By doing so, we can avoid the pending doom of a life lived apart from God and instead walk in the light of His truth, love, and guidance.

Day 31

THE OUTWARD IMAGE

"*Then the king's countenance changed, the joints of his hips were loosened and his knees knocked together.*"

DANIEL 5:6

TODAY, the emphasis on outward appearance has never been more prominent. We have filters on our phones that promise to make us look more youthful and glamorous. Social media platforms are filled with carefully curated images and moments that showcase the very best parts of our lives. Our children are on their best behavior, our vacations are breathtaking, and our achievements are paraded for all to see. But what does this obsession with the outward image mean in the grand scheme of things?

In the Book of Daniel, we find an ancient example of the pursuit of an outward image. King Belshazzar of Babylon hosted a lavish feast, and he spared no expense in showcasing his power and wealth. The city walls were strong, the wine flowed freely, and the vessels from the temple of God were used to toast to the idols of gold and silver. The King's outward image was one of opulence, luxury, and invincibility.

However, that night, Belshazzar's countenance changed, and his thoughts troubled him. His posture wobbled and knees knocked together as he witnessed a mysterious hand writing on the wall, foretelling his impending downfall. In an instant, his carefully crafted outward image was shattered, and he stood exposed as a foolish, arrogant ruler.

This story serves as a powerful reminder that, in life, God's opinion matters most. In 1 Samuel 16:7, we are reminded "Do not look at appearance or physical stature. For the Lord does not see as man sees; for man looks at the outward appearance, but the Lord looks at the heart." King Belshazzar's grandeur couldn't conceal the true condition of his heart, and when God revealed it, he was found lacking.

We often place great importance on titles we hold, possessions we have, or the clothes we wear. We strive to impress our peers and gain their approval, but what about God's perspective? Our worth is not determined by our outward image, but by the value God places on us as His uniquely loved creation. In God's eyes, our true beauty and significance come from who He says we are and not what we have or do.

In life, God's opinion matters most.

As you navigate the world's obsession with outward appearances, remember the story of Belshazzar. Instead of seeking to impress the world, strive to develop an inner heart that seeks to please God alone. Make your life about glorifying Him and reflecting His love to others. Just as King Belshazzar's image crumbled, worldly accolades and appearances will fade, but your value to God remains the same.

In the pursuit of God's approval over the world's applause, you will find genuine fulfillment and lasting significance. Embrace the truth that your worth is not defined by the outward image you project, but by the price Jesus was willing to pay on the cross to purchase your soul.

Day 32
A GOOD REPUTATION

"I have heard of you, that the Spirit of God is in you, and that light and excellent wisdom are found in you."

DANIEL 5:14

IN the bustling and decadent city of Babylon, a chaotic and disturbing scene unfolded within the royal palace. King Belshazzar, heir to Nebuchadnezzar's throne, faced a grave dilemma. His search for wisdom and guidance led him to summon the most renowned counselors and wise men of the land. Yet, none of them could decipher the mysterious writing on the palace wall that had left the king trembling with fear.

Never underestimate what God can do through one person who is fully consecrated to Him.

It is at this point that our attention turns to a man named Daniel. Amid the chaos and uncertainty, he stood as a beacon of hope. Daniel's reputation preceded him, for he was known as a person filled with the Holy Spirit, characterized by godly wisdom and abilities. He was a man of integrity and steadfast faith in the living God.

Daniel's reputation was not built overnight, it was the result of a lifetime of living in accordance with God's commands. His consistent devotion to God had earned him favor and influence even in a foreign land. His reputation had paved the way for a divine appointment with the king.

In the story of Daniel, we are reminded of the timeless truth found in Proverbs 22:1, "A good name is to be chosen rather than great riches; loving favor rather than silver and gold." Daniel's good name and reputation were worth more to him than any position or treasure the king could grant.

As followers of Christ, we are called to maintain a good name and reputation in a world filled with chaos and moral decay. Our character should shine as a light in the darkness, drawing people toward God. Jesus says to His disciples, "Let your light shine before others, that they may see your good deeds and glorify your Father in heaven." (Matthew 5:16) Just as Daniel's reputation opened doors for him to influence a pagan king, our lives of integrity can impact those around us.

Never underestimate what God can do through one person who is fully consecrated to Him. Daniel, one godly person in the heart of Babylon, became a catalyst for change and a vessel through which God displayed His power and wisdom. In the same way, you too can have a tremendous influence and impact for Christ in your circle of friends or sphere of influence.

Let us remember that our reputation is not just about what others think of us, but it reflects our commitment to living a life that honors God. May we strive for a reputation that echoes the words spoken about Daniel: that the Spirit of God is in us, and that light, understanding, and excellent wisdom are found in us through our unshakable faith in the one true God.

Day 33

THE HAND OF GOD

"The God who holds your breath in His hand and owns all your ways, you have not glorified."

DANIEL 5:23

CONSIDER a world where the invisible force of gravity ceases to exist. Chaos would reign as tides would surge uncontrollably, seasons would spiral into disorder, and the very preservation of life on Earth would hang in the balance. Gravity, though unseen, holds the created world together, silently but powerfully governing the cosmic ballet of the universe.

In Daniel 5:23, the Bible draws a parallel between this unseen force and the hand of God, who holds our very breath and governs every aspect of our lives. The contrast is striking — while we may unwittingly take gravity for granted, we must never forget the all-encompassing sovereignty of our Creator.

Our God, who carefully keeps the particles of the universe in their ordained paths, is the same God who intricately designed every facet of your life. He is not a distant observer, He is intimately involved in the details of your existence. Just as gravity works silently to hold the world in equilibrium, God works tirelessly to maintain the order and purpose in your life.

Colossians 1:16-17 declares, "For by Him all things were created that are in heaven and that are on earth, visible and invisible, whether thrones or dominions or principalities or powers. All things were created through Him and for Him. And He is before all things, and holds all things together." Just as God holds the universe in the palm of His hands, He also holds your life together with His grace.

Every breath you take should inhale the grace of God and exhale His praise. Each moment of your life is sustained by His mercy. It is easy to take the simple act of breathing for granted, but when you realize that every breathe is a gift from God, you'll understand the depth of His love and care. Every molecule of your existence is sustained by His goodness.

> ✷
> *Every breath you take should inhale the grace of God and exhale His praise.*

Therefore, as the Creator of the cosmos continues to hold the universe together, we can trust Him to hold together the pieces of our lives. Just as the sun rises faithfully and the tides ebb and flow according to His design, God's promises are reliable. He deserves all our worship and praise, for He not only governs the cosmic order, but also breathes life into our very souls.

The hand of God is a force far greater than gravity, for it holds the universe together and sustains every aspect of our lives. Let us remember that God's sovereignty, just like gravity, is complete and constant. Let us acknowledge His grace with every breath we take and offer Him the praises He is due. His mercy is a profound reason for our worship, and His power is a source of our daily dependence. So, as we marvel at the vastness of His creation, let us also marvel at the personal and loving God who holds us in His hand.

Day 34

A SPIRITUAL RECHARGE

"This is the interpretation. MENE: God has numbered your kingdom, and finished it; TEKEL: You have been weighed and found wanting; PERES: Your kingdom has been divided and given to the Medes and Persians."

DANIEL 5:26-28

NOWADAYS, we marvel at the incredible technology behind electric vehicles. These cars are powered by internal batteries that enable them to run silently and efficiently. However, even the most advanced electric vehicles have one critical limitation: their driving range. They can only go so far before needing to be recharged. Just as these vehicles need periodic recharging, so do our spiritual lives.

Neglecting God's Word leads to a spiritually depleted life.

In Daniel 5, we encounter the dramatic scene where King Belshazzar and the Babylonian Empire fell. It wasn't due to the might of advancing armies or external forces. Instead, it was a consequence of their moral and spiritual decline. God's handwriting on the wall was an unmistakable sign, just as the warning light on an electric vehicle's dashboard indicates the need for a recharge.

The message was clear: MENE — God had numbered the days of Babylon's rule, TEKEL — Babylon had been weighed and found wanting, and PERES — the kingdom would be divided. It's a powerful reminder that our spiritual lives can face a similar fate when we drift away from God's Word and truth.

Jesus Himself cautioned us about the dangers of ignoring His Word. In Matthew 7:26-27, He said, "But everyone who hears these sayings of Mine and does not do them will be like a foolish man who built his house on the sand: and the rain descended, the floods came, and the winds blew and beat on that house; and it fell. And great was its fall."

In the storms of life, without the firm foundation of God's Word, we too can crumble. Just as an electric vehicle without a charge becomes powerless and ineffective, a Christian who neglects the Word of God can become spiritually drained and ineffective in their faith.

A decline or drift from spiritual fervency can lead to apathy and indifference towards God. Eventually, we can find ourselves running on empty, with no internal power to face the challenges of life.

So, let us remember to recharge our spiritual batteries with God's Word daily. Just as electric vehicles are plugged in for a recharge, we should connect with God through prayer and His Word to stay charged and empowered. His Word provides us with the internal power to go the distance for God, to face life's challenges, and to remain faithful in the midst of trials.

Let us not fall into the trap of neglecting God's Word and suffering the consequences of a spiritually depleted life. Instead, make it a daily habit to connect with God, and you'll find that His Word will empower you to navigate life's journey with resilience, faith, and an endless supply of strength.

Day 35

GOD KNOWS YOUR NAME

"That very night Belshazzar, king of the Chaldeans, was slain. And Darius the Mede received the kingdom."

DANIEL 5:30-31

WELCOMING a new baby into the world is a moment filled with immense joy, excitement, and anticipation. It is a time when parents explore countless baby names, each carrying with it a unique meaning and character trait they hope will encapsulate their dreams and aspirations for their precious child. The name chosen becomes the foundation upon which the child's identity will be built.

In the book of Daniel, we find a remarkable story that demonstrates the incredible foreknowledge and sovereignty of God. Belshazzar, the king of Babylon, was reveling in a night of feasting and excess when a mysterious hand appeared, writing on the wall. This supernatural event marked the beginning of the end of Babylon's rule. That very night, King Belshazzar was slain as the Persian Empire took over the kingdom. What makes this story truly remarkable is not just the fall of Babylon, but the fact that God had named the instrument of its fall, Cyrus the Great, 150 years before his birth.

Imagine the depth of God's knowledge and foresight. Just as parents choose names for their children, God chose Cyrus to fulfill a specific purpose long before his existence. In Isaiah 44:28, the Lord says, "That says of Cyrus, 'He is My shepherd, and he shall perform all My pleasure,' saying to Jerusalem, 'You shall be built,' and to the temple, 'Your foundation shall be laid.'"

God not only named Cyrus but also equipped him for the task. In Isaiah 45, the Lord provides a detailed description of how He would empower Cyrus to destroy Babylon and release the Israelites. God's sovereign hand is evident throughout, showing His intimate involvement in shaping the course of history.

The message of God's knowledge goes beyond the story of Cyrus. In Psalm 139:16, we are reminded that God knows every detail about our lives even before we've lived one day. It says, "Your eyes saw my substance, being yet unformed. And in Your book, they all were written, the days fashioned for me, when as yet there were none of them." In the same way, Jeremiah 1:5 tells us that God knew you before He formed you in the womb and ordained all your days.

God knew every detail about your life before you ever lived one day.

The takeaway here is that your life is not a sum of random events and accidents. It's the result of a loving and caring God who personally knows your name and purposefully directs the details of your life. Just as God knew Cyrus and used him for a specific purpose, He knows you and has a plan for your life.

In the joy, excitement, and anticipation of welcoming a new baby, we can see a glimpse of God's anticipation and hope for each of us as His children. So, remember, God knows your name, and He knows your purpose. Trust in Him and let His sovereign hand guide your life, just as He guided Cyrus to fulfill His divine plan.

Day 36

WORKING FOR THE LORD

"This Daniel distinguished himself above the governors because an excellent spirit was in him, and the king gave thought to setting him over the whole realm."

DANIEL 6:3

ON every naval ship each sailor aboard has a unique role and contribution to ensure the success of the mission. From the captain to the cooks, from the navigators to the engineers, each person plays a vital part in achieving the Navy's goals and objectives. Even the most mundane tasks, such as cleaning the deck or maintaining equipment, are crucial to the ship's overall success and should be accomplished with a high level of professionalism and a superior work ethic.

In a similar way, Daniel's life exemplified excellence and dedication in his service to the Lord. He worked diligently in whatever role he was given, knowing that every task was important to God. Whether he was interpreting dreams, managing affairs, or counseling kings, Daniel maintained his integrity and a positive attitude.

Daniel's dependable commitment to his work did not go unnoticed. In fact, the king recognized his excellent character, integrity, and work ethic. The king contemplated setting Daniel over the entire realm because of the remarkable spirit within him. Daniel's excellence was rewarded not only by human authorities, but also by the Lord who honored his convictions.

Colossians 3:23 reminds us that whatever we do, whether in our jobs, studies, or daily tasks, is an opportunity to reflect our commitment and dedication to the Lord. "And whatever you do, do it heartily, as to the Lord and not to men." This verse encourages us to view our work as a means of pleasing God and serving Him through our lives.

There is no job too insignificant when it is accomplished with a heart that seeks to please God.

Through Daniel's example we discover that there is no job too insignificant when it is accomplished with a heart that seeks to please God. Whether you're the CEO of a company or the janitor sweeping the floors, your work can be an act of worship. A Navy ship would never sail smoothly if even one sailor neglects their duties. Likewise, our commitment to excellence impacts the success of our collective mission to serve the Lord.

Today, take a moment to reconsider your motives and attitudes toward your work. Are you working with excellence and dedication, even when no one is watching? Are you approaching your tasks with the mindset of serving the Lord? Let us make a commitment to complete every task with the same dedication and spirit of excellence that defined Daniel's life. In doing so, we not only honor God but also inspire those around us to follow our example. Just as Daniel's excellent spirit set him apart, let your commitment to excellence distinguish you as a faithful servant of the Lord in all that you do.

Day 37
RUSTY RELATIONSHIPS

"So the governors sought to find some charge against Daniel; but they could find no charge or fault because he was faithful, nor was there any error found in him."

DANIEL 6:4

WHEN metal is left outside and exposed to the elements, it slowly but surely develops rust. Over time, if the rust is not removed and the metal remains untreated, those small pockets of rust will gradually grow, causing major corrosion and irreversible damage. In much the same way, jealousy and envy can corrode the human heart and erode relationships, leading to dire consequences.

Humility protects the heart against the corrosive effects of jealousy.

In the book of Daniel, we find a remarkable account of a man who exemplified courageous faith and integrity. Despite Daniel's unblemished character, the leaders of his time grew jealous of him. They couldn't find a legitimate fault or charge against him, but jealousy festered within their hearts. Just as rust silently corrodes metal, jealousy secretly corroded their souls.

Jealousy and envy are like the rust on metal. They start as small pockets of discontent, but when left unchecked, they grow, causing major damage.

These leaders conspired together to destroy Daniel because they couldn't bear the thought of his success and the favor he had found with the king.

Jealousy and selfishness, left unaddressed, can lead to the deterioration and eventual collapse of meaningful relationships. When we harbor jealousy and envy, it's not only our hearts that suffer, but our interactions with others become tainted. Like rust eating away at metal, these negative emotions corrode our ability to see the goodness in others, appreciate their achievements, and support their success.

Daniel's story serves as a powerful reminder of the importance of humility. Humility protects the heart from the corrosive effects of jealousy. Philippians 2:3 encourages us to "do nothing through selfish ambition or conceit, but in lowliness of mind let each esteem others better than themselves." When we humble ourselves, we celebrate the success of others and find joy in their blessings, rather than allowing jealousy to take root.

To guard our hearts against the damaging effects of jealousy and resentment, we must cultivate sincere compassion and genuine appreciation for others. Instead of competing, we should congratulate. Instead of envying, we should encourage. Instead of tearing down, we should build up. We are called to imitate Christ, who exemplified selflessness and love in all He did.

Jealousy, like rust on metal, can corrode our hearts and relationships. Let us learn from the lesson of Daniel and the jealous leaders, choosing humility over envy, and compassion over resentment. Guard your heart against jealousy by sealing your relationships with sincerity and genuine appreciation of others. In doing so, you will find that your life is enriched, your relationships flourish, and you become a reflection of Christ's love and grace in the world.

Day 38
COUNTER CULTURE

"Daniel went home, with his windows open, knelt down on his knees three times that day, and prayed and gave thanks before his God, as was his custom."

DANIEL 6:10

IN the wild, Pacific salmon undertake an awe-inspiring journey that takes them from the vastness of the ocean back to the freshwater homes of their birth. This journey is not for the faint of heart, as these salmon must navigate treacherous obstacles, face deadly predators, and endure exhausting currents as they swim upstream against the fast-flowing rivers and streams. This remarkable odyssey provides us with a powerful analogy for the life of a faithful Christian, particularly as seen through the example of Daniel.

In a world that often contradicts our faith, we must be willing to ride upstream against the prevailing tide of culture.

Daniel lived in a culture vastly different from his own. He found himself in the service of a king who issued a decree that no one should pray to any god except the king. In a world where the current of public opinion dictated conformity, Daniel stood out as a counter-cultural Christian. Like the Pacific salmon, Daniel chose to swim against the tide.

When the law demanded he cease his prayers to God, Daniel refused to compromise. He continued to honor his God by praying openly with his windows open towards Jerusalem. In doing so, he put himself at great risk, just as the salmon expose themselves to danger while pursuing their upstream journey.

What's remarkable about Daniel's defiance is his steadfast commitment to prayer. Even when it was the most dangerous activity at the time, he did not waver in his devotion. This act was not just a mere ritual, it was an act of rebellion against the prevailing culture's demands and a profound demonstration of his allegiance to God. His prayer life was a consistent practice of petitioning God with a heart of submission and thanksgiving.

This aspect of Daniel's life should serve as an example to us as modern Christians. In a world that often contradicts our faith, we too, must be willing to swim upstream, against the flow of the culture. Just as the salmon do not turn back but press on towards their destination, we must continue to live out our faith, even when it's uncomfortable or perilous.

Like Daniel, our greatest allegiance is to God. Just as he defied the king's decree and remained steadfast in his devotion, we must be prepared to stand up for our beliefs, even when it goes against the prevailing culture. The culture may flow in one direction, but our faith propels us in another.

In a world that constantly tempts us to conform and compromise our beliefs, we can draw inspiration from Daniel's commitment to prayer and his refusal to bow to the cultural pressures. We can choose to live as counter-cultural Christians, just as the Pacific salmon choose to swim upstream, undeterred by the obstacles and dangers. Our strength, like Daniel's, is found in the hope and promises of God as our defender and protector.

Day 39
GOD IS ALWAYS WATCHING

"That Daniel, who is one of the captives from Judah, does not show due regard for the decree that you have signed, but makes his petition three times a day."

DANIEL 6:13

IN the realm of espionage and covert operations, elite military forces employ an array of tactics to gather intelligence, often lurking in the shadows, undetected. These skilled individuals are capable of infiltrating the inner circles of unsuspecting targets, gaining insight into their conversations, and unraveling their secret plans. This analogy of vigilant surveillance techniques gives us a remarkable perspective on the events surrounding Daniel 6:13, where we discover that even when we think no one is ever looking, God is always watching.

The story of Daniel in the lion's den unfolds against a backdrop of jealousy and conspiracy among the leaders of the kingdom. Like a well-orchestrated covert mission, they secretly conspired to trap Daniel, exploiting his extraordinary commitment to God as their way in. Their objective: to expose him breaking the law by continuing to pray to the one true God. They set up a spying operation that would catch him in the act, just as elite operatives catch their targets off-guard.

In this situation, we see Daniel as the unsuspecting target, a man whose devout faith and loyalty to God made him a prime subject for surveillance.

Despite knowing the consequences, he chose to continue praying and seeking God's mercies and favor, even when the eyes of the world were upon him. He understood that pleasing the Lord was far more critical than pleasing people.

In the same way, we should remember that God's watchful eyes are always upon us, even when we believe no one is observing our actions and motives. Proverbs 5:21 reminds us, "For the ways of man are before the eyes of the Lord, and He ponders all his paths." Just as the conspirators meticulously scrutinized Daniel's every move, God examines our lives with an attentive gaze, penetrating to the depths of our hearts.

Daniel's godly character and integrity serve as a powerful reminder and encouragement for us all. He demonstrated that our lives are best lived in a constant pursuit of pleasing the Lord. When we face scrutiny, opposition, or even the watchful eyes of those who may wrongfully accuse us, we can take inspiration from Daniel. His commitment to God teaches us that, ultimately, it is God's approval that matters most.

Even when we think no one is ever looking, God is always watching.

In the end, Daniel's unyielding faith did not go unnoticed by God. Just as He delivered Daniel from the lion's den, God is faithful to protect and guide those who steadfastly seek Him. So, as we navigate our own journeys through life's challenges and adversities, let us remember that God is always watching, and His favor is the greatest reward we can ever receive.

Day 40
A GOSPEL GLIMPSE

"Then a stone was laid on the mouth of the den, and the king sealed it with his own signet ring, that the purpose concerning Daniel might not be changed."

DANIEL 6:17

IN the early 1990s, the world witnessed the birth of a pop culture phenomenon called "Magic Eye." These seemingly ordinary pictures, known as autostereograms, held a remarkable secret — a hidden 3D image. By adjusting the angle of your stare beyond the surface pattern, your brain automatically constructed the picture within a picture. Just as these illusions held secrets waiting to be unlocked, every page of Scripture points to the person of Jesus, waiting for the right perspective to reveal the three-dimensional image of the gospel.

In the narrative of Daniel chapter 6, we find a powerful analogy to this hidden message of the gospel and an incredible parallel to Jesus. First, consider the character of Daniel. Just as every detail in a Magic Eye picture contributes to the hidden image, every detail in Daniel's life points to the perfection of Jesus. Daniel was blameless, living a life of righteousness before God, and so was Jesus, who was sinless, embodying perfect holiness.

Furthermore, Daniel faced opposition from jealous leaders who sought to destroy him. Likewise, Jesus was wrongly accused and betrayed by those who envied Him. In the same way that Daniel was forced to bow down and worship an idol, Jesus was tempted to do the same by Satan in the wilderness, but He remained steadfast in His devotion to God.

As Daniel prayed to his God, so did Jesus in the garden of Gethsemane before His betrayal, submitting to the Father's will even in the face of impending suffering and death. When Daniel's fate hung in the balance, King Darius wrestled with his decision. Similarly, Pontius Pilate, the Roman governor of Judea, struggled with his conscience as he attempted to release Jesus.

Every page of Scripture points to the person of Jesus.

Remarkably, just as king Darius' command could not be changed, God's righteous law against sin could not be altered. A perfect sacrifice was required. Daniel was thrown into a den of lions, and a stone was rolled over the entrance. In the same way, Jesus was sent to His death on the cross, and His body was placed in a tomb, sealed with a great stone.

But, just as Daniel emerged from certain death unharmed and was highly exalted in the kingdom, Jesus triumphantly resurrected from the dead and ascended to the right hand of the Father in heaven. Through His resurrection, He offers eternal life to all who place their trust in Him.

When we look at the two-dimensional pages of Scripture with the eyes of faith, we begin to see the three-dimensional image of the gospel of Jesus Christ. Just as Magic Eye pictures reveal hidden beauty when viewed correctly, the Bible unveils the beauty of Christ when we read it with a gospel lens. May we fix our gaze on Jesus, for in Him, we find not an illusion but the ultimate reality - the way, the truth, and the life.

Day 41

A RESTLESS SOUL

> "Now the king went to his palace and spent the night fasting; and no musicians were brought before him. Also, his sleep went from him."
>
> **DANIEL 6:18**

WE'VE all been there, haven't we? Those restless nights when sleep seems to elude us. It's a common affliction that plagues millions, leaving them tossing and turning in the stillness of the night. Recent studies have provided valuable insights into how to attain that elusive good night's sleep: sticking to a consistent sleep schedule, creating a restful environment, avoiding large meals and drinks, managing worries, and removing electronic devices. Yet, even with all these tips, there are moments when the mind simply refuses to rest.

The search for true peace is not found in the absence of crisis, but in the presence of Jesus.

In the book of Daniel, we find a powerful illustration of such a restless soul in King Darius. His sleepless night was not caused by caffeine or a noisy neighbor, but rather by the weight of a decision he had made — a decision that filled him with deep regret and anxiety. He had reluctantly condemned Daniel, his trusted advisor and friend, to be cast into the den of hungry lions. Regret gnawed at his conscience, depriving him of the peace he sought.

Our lives often mirror King Darius's sleepless night. We, too, are haunted by trials, anxieties, and regrets. The decisions we make, the trials we face, and the burdens we carry can leave us in a state of sleeplessness, our minds consumed by relentless worries. Yet, even in the darkest hours, there is hope. That's because true peace is not the absence of crisis, but the presence of Jesus. When worry overwhelms us, we can still experience a deep peace and rest in our souls because of Jesus' faithful promises.

Scripture reminds us in Philippians 4:6-7: "Be anxious for nothing, but in everything by prayer and supplication with thanksgiving, present your requests to God, and the peace of God which surpasses all understanding will guard your heart and mind in Christ Jesus." In our times of unrest, we can take refuge in prayer, laying our burdens at the feet of the One who can calm the turmoil within us. Jesus even extends this invitation to us in Matthew 11:28: "Come to Me, all you who are weary and are heavy burdened, and I will give you rest for your souls." In Him, we find the ultimate source of rest, even in the face of our deepest regrets and anxieties.

For every regret and trial that keeps us awake at night, Jesus offers the healing power and calming presence needed for our restless souls. He bore our burdens on the cross, offering us forgiveness and restoration. In Him, our past regrets and present worries are treated with His loving care.

King Darius's sleepless night was a result of his regret and worry, much like our own restless moments. The good news is that we don't have to face these sleepless nights alone. In Christ, we find solace, rest, and peace. His promises assure us that we can experience rest, even in the midst of life's trials. So, when the cares of life keep you awake at night, remember to take your anxieties to Him in prayer, and allow His peace to guard your heart and mind. Jesus offers open arms to give us the rest we so desperately need.

Day 42

DIVINE DELIVERANCE

"The king was exceedingly glad. So Daniel was taken up out of the den, and no injury whatever was found on him because he believed in his God."

DANIEL 6:23

HAVE you ever watched a daredevil perform an astonishing stunt, risking life and limb to amaze an audience? We often find ourselves captivated by their audacity to defy the odds and face danger head-on. Whether it's tightrope walking across Niagara Falls or jumping a canyon on a rocket-powered motorcycle, these thrill-seekers leave us in awe, as they emerge unscathed from the brink of disaster. But there is one tale that surpasses all these daring exploits — an account that not only defies human understanding but leaves us astounded by the powerful protection of God.

In the book of Daniel, we find a story of a man who faced a perilous challenge that made the feats of daredevils seem like child's play. Daniel, a man of courageous faith, was thrown into a den of hungry lions by the decree of King Darius. It was a night fraught with danger, and the odds were heavily stacked against him. Yet, miraculously, the claws and jaws of those fierce and ravenous beasts were no match for the raw power and awe of God.

Just like those amazed onlookers at a daredevil stunt show, King Darius watched in utter disbelief, as Daniel emerged unharmed from the lion's den. The king's heart must have skipped a beat as he realized that the man who had been thrown to his doom was now alive and well. Daniel's miraculous escape was not the result of months of careful planning. It was a divine deliverance, a clear demonstration of God's mighty hand at work.

In our own lives, we may face moments that seem as treacherous as a lion's den. It might be a health crisis, financial difficulties, or any number of challenges that threaten to engulf us. In those times, we often feel like we're walking a tightrope over the abyss, with the audience of our fears and doubts watching closely. But here's the good news: just as God delivered Daniel from the clutches of the hungry lions, He promises to deliver and protect the righteous from harm and trouble.

God promises His protection and peace when life is poised to pounce and tear you to pieces.

The Scriptures remind us, "The righteous cry out and the Lord hears them and delivers them from all their troubles." (Psalm 34:17) When we seek the Lord, He delivers us from all our fears because "God is our hiding place, rock, fortress, and refuge." (Psalm 91:1-2) He surrounds us with songs of deliverance, just as He surrounded Daniel with angelic protection.

So, if you find yourself in the midst of life's trials, remember Daniel's divine deliverance. When it seems like the world is poised to pounce and tear you to pieces, trust in the power and peace of God. He is your refuge, your rock, and your fortress. Like Daniel, you too can emerge unharmed, to the shock and amazement of those who witness the miraculous work of God in your life. Your faith in Him will be your tightrope across the chasm, your rocket-powered escape from danger, and your assurance that God's protection and peace will see you through any perilous situation.

Day 43

DREAMS AND VISIONS

"In the first year of Belshazzar king of Babylon, Daniel had a dream and visions while on his bed."

DANIEL 7:1

IN the vast expanse of a desert, where the scorching sun meets the arid sands, an intriguing phenomenon unfolds. As the searing heat refracts light from the unforgiving surface, a deceptive mirage emerges. In this barren landscape, our eyes play tricks on us, making us believe that a watery oasis lies just ahead, only to discover that it was a mere illusion.

God can speak through dreams and visions, but their meaning will never contradict the revelation of His written Word.

Much like this desert mirage, God bestowed upon Daniel a remarkable ability to see and understand complex visions and dreams. The book of Daniel, in particular, paints a vivid picture of his prophetic experiences. These visions were not like the deceptive mirages of the desert, but were divinely inspired glimpses into the grand unveiling of God's divine plan.

Throughout Scripture we see God use a multitude of avenues to communicate with His people. The primary channel, of course, is the Word of God, the Bible, which provides the timeless foundation for our faith. Additionally, the Holy Spirit within us guides our hearts and minds, providing insight and revelation. God often uses godly counsel from family and friends, external circumstances, and, indeed, dreams and visions.

In Daniel's case, these dreams and visions were not mere illusions, but divine revelations meant to convey God's message. They were keys that unlocked the mysteries of the present and the future, revealing God's plan for His people. Daniel's openness and receptiveness to these unique forms of communication allowed him to serve God with sincere faith.

The Scriptures reminds us that in the last days, "God will pour out His Spirit on all flesh. Sons and daughters will prophesy, old men will dream dreams, and young men will see visions." (Joel 2:28) This promise was fulfilled when the Church was birthed in the Book of Acts and assures us that God desires an intimate relationship with us, speaking to us in diverse ways, revealing His will for our lives, and giving us insights into His plans.

However, we must heed a crucial warning: while God can speak to us through dreams and visions, their meaning will never contradict the revelation of His written Word. The Bible is our unchanging foundation and the plumb line by which we measure all spiritual experiences. Dreams and visions, like all aspects of our faith, must align with the truth of God's Word.

In life, we are encouraged to see and hear God with eyes of faith that perceive past fuzzy illusions. We must tune our ears to the voice of God, seeking His guidance through the Word, the Spirit, and even dreams and visions. Let us embrace these divine interactions with humility, discernment, and a heart inclined to obey God's will. As we follow His guidance, may our lives become a testament to His faithfulness and our trust in His perfect plan.

Day 44

FUTURE KINGDOMS

"And four great beasts came up from the sea, diverse one from another."

DANIEL 7:3

IMAGINE yourself in a dimly lit room, eagerly watching a skilled magician perform a mesmerizing act. The magician's hands move with precision, using diversion and sleight of hand techniques to create an illusion that leaves you in surprised curiosity. One moment, a card has disappeared, and the next, it appears in your pocket, the whole room filled with awe and wonder. It's a captivating performance, but one built on deception and tricks.

In the book of Daniel, we encounter a different kind of revelation, a vision that transcends mere human tricks. Daniel's vision, accurately predicted and foretold with specific details the rise and fall of powerful world empires. These prophecies, unlike the magician's illusion, are not built on deception, but are validated by the fulfillment of ancient human history.

Daniel's vision unfolded like the magician's act but with divine accuracy. The four great beasts rising from the sea symbolized the Babylonian, Medo-Persian, Greek, and Roman empires. Each beast was diverse from the others, just as these empires were unique in their rise and fall, and their distinct characteristics left a lasting mark on history.

The Babylonians, symbolized by the lion, were known for their strength and dominance. The bear represented the Medo-Persian Empire, with one side stronger than the other, reflecting the dual leadership of the Medes and Persians. The leopard, with wings like a bird, depicted the swiftness of Alexander the Great's conquests during the Greek Empire. The fourth beast, with iron teeth and ten horns, signified the formidable Roman Empire.

Human kingdoms, as history reveals, have risen and fallen, just like the magician's tricks that come to an end once the secret is revealed. But the Word of God, as seen in Daniel's vision, stands as a testament to the precision of his prophecy.

The magician's illusion may leave you in surprise, but it is temporary, just as these earthly kingdoms were. Ultimately, human kingdoms will fall to the rise of a divine King. The Kingdom of Heaven, promised by God, will endure forever through the rule and reign of Jesus Christ as the King of kings and Lord of lords.

> *Human kingdoms will fall to the rise of a Divine King.*

As we reflect on Daniel's vision, we are reminded that God's Word is a reliable and unerring source of truth. Just as God's Word accurately predicted past historical events, we can trust that unfulfilled biblical prophecy concerning the return of Jesus will come to pass in the unveiling of God's divine timeline.

In a world where illusion and deception may surround us, let us hold fast to the everlasting truth that God's Word reveals. His Kingdom is eternal, and His promises are sure. The rise and fall of earthly empires are mere shadows compared to the radiant and enduring glory of the Kingdom of Heaven, where God's divine King will reign for all eternity.

Day 45

HELP ON HIGH

"I watched till thrones were put in place, and the Ancient of Days was seated; His garment was white as snow, the hair of His head was like pure wool."

DANIEL 7:9

IMAGINE being a castaway, lost at sea, with no land in sight. You're adrift in the vast expanse of the ocean, and your only hope lies in sending out distress signals, hoping against hope that someone will hear your call and come to your rescue. The isolation, the despair, the uncertainty — it's a harrowing experience. But then, on the distant horizon, you see it — an airplane or a rescue helicopter responding to your SOS messages. In that moment, your despair turns to joy because help is on the way.

Just one peek of heaven brightens every bleak condition.

In the book of Daniel, we find a scene of distress, despair, and hope — a vision that left Daniel distraught. He saw the destruction of nations, the persecution of God's people, and the defiance of God's authority by earthly rulers. The chaos and turmoil of the world around him were overwhelming. But in the midst of his distress, God gave Daniel a glimpse of His heavenly throne. Daniel's vision of the "Ancient of Days" seated on a fiery throne, with garments white as snow, brought him hope. In that moment, he realized that God was sovereign, even in the face of earthly chaos. The distress of the world was no match for the glory of God's eternal reign.

Daniel's experience is not unique. The prophet Isaiah, during a time of uncertainty and turmoil in Israel, "Saw the Lord seated on the throne, and the train of His robe filled the temple with glory." (Isaiah 6:1) John, the last surviving apostle, also received a revelation of the throne room of heaven, describing it as filled with rainbows, lightnings, thunderings, flames of fire, and a sea of crystal glass (Revelation 4:2-6). In the midst of their despair and distress, these faithful servants of God were granted visions of the Almighty on His heavenly throne.

Just as castaways lift their eyes to the horizon, desperate for rescue, we too can lift our eyes on high. Our distress signals are our prayers, sent heavenward, seeking the One who hears and responds. Psalm 121:1-2 reminds us, "I will lift up my eyes to the hills—from whence comes my help? My help comes from the Lord, who made heaven and earth." When the circumstances of life become increasingly distressing, when the world around us appears chaotic, and when our personal challenges overwhelm us, remember that God is infinitely above our plight.

God, the Ancient of Days, reigns on the throne, and He is our ever-present help. Just one peek of heaven brightens every bleak condition. When you find yourself in the depths of despair, send up your distress signal in prayer. Look to the heavens, for your help comes from the One who made heaven and earth. He hears your cries, calms your fears, and rescues you from the darkest storms.

Day 46

ALL RISE

"A thousand thousands ministered to Him; ten thousand times ten thousand stood before Him."

DANIEL 7:10A

IN the solemn and sacred halls of justice, we often witness a profound moment of reverence and anticipation. As the courtroom falls into hushed silence, a powerful ceremony begins — the judge takes their seat on the judgment bench, and all rise. It is an awe-inspiring display of respect for the authority of the court, a moment when the gravity of the situation becomes unmistakable, as the defendant pleads their case before an attentive jury.

This image paints a vivid picture of the scene that unfolds in the vision of the prophet Daniel, where he glimpses the heavenly courtroom of the Ancient of Days. The imagery reflects the breathtaking awe and seriousness of God's court. Thousands upon thousands stand in attendance, as they wait their turn to take the witness stand. This is a moment of divine reckoning, where every action and thought of humanity is laid bare before the Almighty.

But here's the profound truth that this vision of the heavenly courtroom unveils: when we, as humanity, stand before a holy and just God, we are all found guilty. 1 John 2:1-2 reminds us that sin stains every soul. Our actions, our thoughts, our very nature bear witness against us. We are left without defense, evidence, or an alibi sufficient to prove our innocence. The weight of our guilt presses upon us as we come face to face with perfect justice.

In the courtroom of heaven, it seems as though there is no hope, no escape from the righteous judgment of God. Our sins are counted against us, and the consequences of our rebellion are severe. But here is where the message of the Gospel shines with brilliant clarity — the only way to escape God's righteous judgment is to accept Jesus as our sinful payment. He becomes our Advocate, standing before the heavenly court on our behalf.

At the cross of Calvary, Jesus, the Lamb of God, willingly bore the weight of our guilt. He paid the penalty for our sins through His merciful sacrifice. The justice of God was satisfied by His selfless act of love, and those who repent and turn to Jesus find their sins washed away. Their guilty records are expunged, and they are set free from the penalty of sin and death.

The cross of Calvary is the place where God's justice is satisfied by Jesus' merciful sacrifice.

This is the heart of the Gospel — the miraculous exchange of our guilt for His righteousness. When we place our faith in Jesus, we are justified by His grace, and God's judgment is replaced with His mercy. The courtroom of heaven becomes a place of redemption, where the guilty are declared innocent, not because of their works, but because of God's grace through faith in Jesus Christ.

So, as we stand in the presence of the Almighty, let us remember the vision of Daniel's courtroom in heaven. All rise, for God's justice is absolute, but His mercy is boundless. Let us acknowledge our need for Jesus, who pleads our case and offers us forgiveness, redemption, and eternal life. The cross of calvary is the place where God's justice and mercy intersect, and it is the place where we find hope, salvation, and everlasting joy.

Day 47

HEAVENLY BOOKSHELF

"... The court was seated and the books were opened."

DANIEL 7:10B

AS children, many of us experienced the joy and excitement of using invisible ink to send secret messages to our friends. Those seemingly blank pages held a hidden world, known only to the sender and the receiver. To reveal the concealed message, we had to expose it to a specific light or heat source, bringing forth the once-hidden words. In much the same way, Daniel's vision of the heavenly courtroom scene in the Book of Daniel reminds us of the hidden and revealed aspects of God's divine plan.

In Daniel's vision, he saw a majestic throne room with thousands upon thousands attending to the Almighty God. The court was seated, and the books were opened. This remarkable imagery tells us that there is a record, a divine account of our lives, meticulously maintained by God Himself. This heavenly library contains references to certain books on God's bookshelf, two of which are particularly intriguing.

The first book, the "Book of Remembrance," can be found in the Book of Malachi (Malachi 3:16). In it, God keeps a personal journal of every time we speak with others about His faithfulness, love, and grace. It is as if every act of sharing the Gospel, every act of kindness, and every moment of love is recorded in this special volume. Our seemingly invisible deeds, like the hidden messages of our childhood, are made visible in the presence of God.

The second book is the "Lamb's Book of Life," which is mentioned in the Book of Revelation (Revelation 3:5). This book contains the names of those whose sins have been forgiven by the precious blood of Jesus Christ. Unlike the invisible ink messages, the names in the Lamb's Book of Life were not written in pencil or black ink, but in the permanent red blood of Jesus.

The Book of Life was not written in erasable pencil, but in the permanent red markings of Jesus' sacrifice.

You see, the beauty of these heavenly books lies in their permanence. While our earthly deeds may fade with time, God's record of our lives remains eternally secure. The Lamb's Book of Life contains the names of those who have received God's salvation, and those names will never be blotted out. When you accept Jesus as your Savior, your name is forever recorded.

The Book of Remembrance is a testament to our faithful witness, a record of the impact we have in sharing the Good News of Christ. Every time we meditate on and celebrate the goodness of God on this earth, we are adding a page to this heavenly journal. God sees and knows our names, and He records our acts of love, service, and praise.

In a world where our words and actions often seem unimportant, remember that God sees and cherishes every moment you spend in His service. He knows your name, and it is securely recorded in the Lamb's Book of Life. Your salvation is assured, not by invisible ink, but by the permanent markings of the finished work of Jesus Christ on the cross. Rest in the knowledge that your life and salvation are eternally written in the crimson ink of His sacrifice and that He is the author and finisher of your faith.

Day 48

THE LION AND THE LAMB

"I was watching in the night visions, and behold, One like the Son of Man, coming with the clouds of heaven! He came near to the Ancient of Days."

DANIEL 7:13

HAVE you ever had the privilege of visiting a zoo and standing in awe before the enclosure of a majestic lion? If you have, you understand the feeling of wonder, the sense of power, and the recognition that you are witnessing a truly remarkable and fearsome creature. Lions are often regarded as the kings of the jungle, and their presence alone commands respect and admiration. The piercing eyes, massive teeth, ferocious claws, and the rumbling roar of a lion all symbolize the epitome of power.

Jesus is not only the Lamb who bore our sins, but also the Lion who forever reigns.

In the book of Daniel, we find a vision that beautifully combines the awe-inspiring imagery of a lion with the divine revelation of the Son of Man. Daniel's vision transports us to the heavenly realm where he sees the Son of Man approaching the throne of God. This vision is a foretelling of Jesus Christ, the Messiah, who would come to fulfill His role as the conquering King of kings. Just as a lion is majestic and mighty, so is the Son of Man, who approaches the Ancient of Days with clouds of heaven.

In the Bible, Jesus is described using various titles, and one of the most powerful is "the Lion of the tribe of Judah." This title speaks to His authority, signifying that He is the ultimate ruler. He is the one who will bring justice, establish His eternal kingdom, and conquer all opposition. Just like the lion is the king of the jungle, Jesus is the King of all creation.

However, Jesus also carries another title, one that may seem paradoxical at first — "the Lamb of God." During His earthly life and ministry, Jesus came as a suffering servant, willingly offering Himself as a sacrifice for our sins. He humbled Himself, taking on the role of the Lamb, to bear the weight of our iniquities on the cross. His sacrifice on the cross, like the shedding of a lamb's blood in the Old Testament, atoned for our sins, reconciling us to God.

In Daniel's vision, the dual nature of Christ is unveiled. He is the Lion of Judah, the conquering King, and He is the Son of Man, the humble Lamb who identifies with our weaknesses. The Lion and the Lamb coexist in the same person, demonstrating the incredible depth of Christ's character. He is both the powerful, majestic ruler and the compassionate, sacrificial Savior.

As followers of Jesus, we find encouragement in this truth. Jesus has fulfilled His role as the Lamb of God, offering us salvation. And just as He promised, He will return as the conquering King. As in the vision, He will come with the clouds of heaven, and every knee shall bow before Him. Our Savior is not only the Lamb who bore our sins, but also the Lion who forever reigns.

Like a lion at the zoo, the vision of the Son of Man should inspire awe and reverence. Jesus, the Lion and the Lamb, embodies both the strength and majesty of a lion and the gentleness and sacrifice of a lamb. He is the King of kings who suffered for our sins and will return in glory. Let us hold fast to our faith, for Jesus is our Savior and King, now and forevermore.

Day 49

A COUNTERFEIT CHRIST

"The same horn was making war against the saints and prevailing against them until the Ancient of Days came, a judgment was made in favor of the saints, and the time came for the saints to possess the kingdom."

DANIEL 7:21-22

COUNTERFEIT money has become more difficult to catch. That's because counterfeiters go to great lengths to produce fake currency that closely resembles genuine bills. They meticulously craft copies with similar features, using advanced printing techniques. To combat this, financial institutions and authorities train fraud investigators to identify counterfeit money, but what's their secret? They closely examine and handle authentic bills regularly, so they can easily spot the counterfeit.

In the book of Daniel, we encounter a vision that reveals a different kind of counterfeit — the rise of a "little horn." This "little horn" represents a person often referred to as the "Antichrist." As the end times unfold, this counterfeit christ emerges, deceiving many with the illusion of divinity. The Antichrist may appear to be a messianic figure, but in reality, their actions demonstrate that they are the opposite, the adversary, and a counterfeit.

The Antichrist's deceptive nature mirrors the counterfeit money, closely resembling the genuine, but far from the real deal. This individual's blasphemous speech and hostile actions stand in stark contrast to everything

Jesus stands for. The Antichrist seeks to usurp Christ's authority and deceive people into following a false messiah.

> *The best way to recognize counterfeit Christianity is to closely familiarize yourself with the genuine Christ.*

The Bible warns that the Antichrist will not only deceive many, but will also persecute the Church of Jesus Christ during a time of great tribulation. This counterfeit Christ will attempt to lead believers astray, causing confusion and chaos.

In our world and culture, we can already see the spirit of antichrist at work. It seeks to deceive people into pursuing and believing things that are contrary to God's Word and the ministry and works of Jesus. False doctrines, false prophets, and counterfeit Christianity have infiltrated many aspects of our lives. Just as with counterfeit money, it is essential to be vigilant and discerning.

The best way to recognize counterfeit Christianity is to closely familiarize yourself with the genuine Christ. Handle Him regularly through faith, immerse yourself in the truth of God's Word, and stay close to Him. As you grow in your knowledge of Jesus, you will be better equipped to discern the counterfeit distractions and deceptions that exist in the world.

Counterfeit currency may appear convincing at first glance, but those well-versed in authentic currency can easily spot the fake. Similarly, by immersing ourselves in the true teachings of Jesus, we can recognize and resist the deceptive allure of counterfeit christs. The genuine Christ is the only one who can truly satisfy our souls, offering us eternal life, hope, and salvation.

Day 50
GOD'S UNEXPECTED WILL

"Then I lifted my eyes and saw a ram which had two horns, and the two horns were high; but one was higher than the other, and the higher one came up last."

DANIEL 8:3

IN 1980, an iconic moment in U.S. sports history unfolded. A group of young, inexperienced, and largely unknown college hockey players faced the formidable Soviet Union's team, a hockey powerhouse that had won gold in six of the previous seven Winter Olympics. The "Miracle on Ice" was born when the unlikely underdog Americans achieved the impossible and defeated the seemingly unbeatable Soviets. The commentator's famous line captured the essence of the moment: "Do you believe in miracles? Yes!"

> *God can use unlikely people to accomplish His incredibly miraculous plan.*

This incredible underdog victory reminds us that God often works in unexpected ways. In the Book of Daniel, we find a vision that speaks to the unexpected will of God. In Daniel 8:3, we read about a ram with two horns, symbolizing the kings of Media and Persia. This vision reveals the rise and fall of powerful empires, demonstrating how God weaves His redemptive plan through the course of history, guiding events towards the fulfillment of His intended purpose.

God's plan is not always evident at first glance. He often uses unlikely figures to fulfill His purposes. In the case of Daniel's prophetic visions, we see that ungodly rulers, like King Cyrus of the Persian Empire and Alexander the Great of the Greek Empire, were instrumental in the unfolding of biblical prophecy. These men, though imperfect and ungodly, were used by God to accomplish His extraordinary plan.

Romans 8:28 reminds us, "And we know that in all things God works for the good of those who love Him, who have been called according to His purpose." This verse assures us that even in the face of difficult people or circumstances, God can use the unexpected as a source for accomplishing His extraordinary plan in our lives. Just as the unlikely American hockey players achieved the miracle on ice, God can use the unpredictable difficulties and challenges we face to fulfill His purpose.

We can have trust and hope in the unlikely ways God fulfills His purpose and will for our lives. Just as the victory of the American hockey team was met with cheers of amazement and joy, we can praise God for the miraculous ways He works in our lives. Our faith and belief in His ability to bring about the unexpected can serve as a source of comfort and inspiration as we navigate the ups and downs of life.

In times of uncertainty and when facing seemingly insurmountable odds, remember that God's plan is not bound by human limitations. He is the author of miracles, and He can use the most unlikely people and circumstances to fulfill His will. Let us have faith, trust, and hope in the unexpected will of God, for in His perfect timing, He can bring about the most miraculous and awe-inspiring victories in our lives.

Day 51
AN ACCURATE ACCOUNT

"'How long will the vision be, concerning the daily sacrifices and the transgression of desolation?' And he said to me, 'For two thousand three hundred days.'"

DANIEL 8:13-14

LIFE can often be compared to a complex jigsaw puzzle, with countless pieces of various shapes and sizes, each one seemingly disconnected from the other. Just like piecing together a puzzle requires precision and care, the same can be said about the intricate design of our lives. In the book of Daniel, we find a remarkable analogy that reveals God's attention to detail and His divine plan for the future.

In Daniel 8:13-14, we are presented with a detailed vision that baffled the prophet. The vision spoke of daily sacrifices being taken away, a transgression of desolation, and the sanctuary and the host being trampled underfoot. The pieces of this prophetic puzzle seemed confusing, but God had carefully arranged them in a way that would ultimately reveal His plan.

As history unfolded, the pieces of this prophecy began to align with astonishing accuracy. The "little horn" in Daniel's vision represented a future Syrian leader named Antiochus Epiphanes. He invaded Judea, persecuted the Israelites, and desecrated the temple, exactly as foretold by God in Daniel's dream. Every piece of this prophecy fell into place, just like a perfectly cut jigsaw piece that fits snugly into the larger picture.

What makes this prophecy even more astonishing is the precise timing. God provided an accurate account of the exact number of days (2,300 days) that the temple would be desecrated before the Maccabean Revolt would restore the temple and its daily sacrifices. To this day, the Jewish people commemorate these events every year during Hanukkah. This level of detail highlights God's omniscience and His control over time itself.

Just as God orchestrated every detail of Daniel's vision with precision, He is also personally arranging the pieces of your life. He sees how every relationship, activity, achievement, and even failure fit together in the grand picture of your life. You are not an accident or a random collection of events. God is arranging the pieces of your life in just the right way to bring about your good and His glory.

> God is arranging the pieces of your life in just the right way to bring about your good and His glory.

Jeremiah 29:11 reminds us of God's intentionality: "For I know the plans I have for you, declares the Lord, plans to prosper you and not to harm you, plans to give you hope and a future." Just like the pieces of Daniel's prophecy came together at the appointed time, the events in your life today are important pieces in the person God is making you into for the future.

As you reflect on the accuracy of God's plans in the prophecy of Daniel, be encouraged that the same God who ordered every piece of that puzzle is orchestrating every aspect of your life. Every relationship, every opportunity, every challenge — they all have their place in God's grand design. Trust in His wisdom and sovereignty, for He is arranging the pieces of your life to accomplish His purpose and to reveal His glory.

Day 52

GODLY WISDOM

> "And I heard a man's voice who called and said, 'Gabriel, make this man understand the vision.'"
>
> **DANIEL 8:16**

IMAGINE the tender scene of a loving parent and their overly inquisitive young child. This child is a seeker of knowledge, their curiosity knows no bounds. They constantly ask questions, seeking to understand the world around them. With wide eyes and an insatiable appetite for knowledge, they approach their parents, time and time again, confident that their loving caregivers will provide answers with unceasing care and compassion.

Now, picture Daniel, a faithful servant of God, who found himself in a situation much like this in his own way. In the Bible, we read about a time when he witnessed a troubling and disturbing vision about future events. He was very distraught and concerned because of the complexities of what he saw, just like an inquisitive child, perplexed by the mysteries of the world around them.

In his moment of distress and uncertainty, Daniel turned to God. He sought wisdom and discernment, much like a young child seeks understanding from their parents. Just as a loving parent responds to their child's questions with patience and grace, God provided Daniel with understanding to soothe his worries and anxieties. The lesson is clear: God provides clarity to those confused by life's profound mysteries.

This promise from Daniel's experience extends to us today. We, too, can approach our heavenly Father when we are troubled by uncertain circumstances and events. There is no mystery too great for God to solve. As it is written in the book of James, "If any of you lacks wisdom, let him ask of God, who gives to all liberally and without reproach, and it will be given to him." (James 1:5)

> *God provides clarity to those confused by life's profound mysteries.*

Godly wisdom is not merely an intellectual gift, it carries with it the characteristics described in the book of James — pure, peaceable, gentle, willing to yield, full of mercy and good fruits, and without hypocrisy. It is a wisdom that brings tranquility to our troubled hearts and guides use through moments of crisis and confusion.

In light of these truths, remember that Godly wisdom is available to those who ask. While we may not receive every specific detail to our questions, we can have hope and assurance that our heavenly Father will lead and guide us through every twist and turn of life's mysterious path. Just as a loving parent imparts knowledge to their child, our heavenly Father imparts wisdom to us when we come to Him with open and trusting hearts.

In times of confusion, uncertainty, and distress, remember that you can turn to God, your loving Father, who holds the key to unlocking the mysteries of your life. Seek His wisdom, trust in His guidance, and find peace in the assurance that He is with you, always ready to answer your questions with unceasing care, patience, and gentle compassion.

Day 53
DOUBLE VISION

"And he said, 'Look, I am making known to you what shall happen in the latter time of the indignation; for at the appointed time the end shall be.'"

DANIEL 8:19

IMAGINE waking up each day, struggling to see clearly. Some of us might be familiar with the inconvenience of vision problems — nearsightedness, farsightedness, or even the frustrating blur of double vision. Fortunately, optometrists exist to diagnose and prescribe corrective lenses, bringing clarity to our world.

Similarly, Daniel's vision in Chapter 8 can be seen as a divine lens, correcting the blurred vision of the future. Biblical prophecy, like a pair of corrective lenses, sharpens our focus on events both near and far, unveiling God's sovereign plan for humanity.

Biblical prophecy has near and far historical relevancy.

The analogy of corrective lenses becomes even more profound when we consider progressive lenses. Just as these lenses enable clear vision for both near and far distances, Daniel's vision transcends time, revealing events on the horizon and in the distant future. In this case, biblical prophecy has near and far historical relevancy.

Daniel's vision unveils the rise and fall of empires — the Medes, Persians, and Greeks — all seen through the lens of God's providence. The destruction of Jerusalem, persecution of the Israelites, and the desecration of the temple are vividly depicted. Yet, simultaneously, the vision stretches forward, anticipating a time when an antichrist figure will emerge during the great tribulation.

In essence, Daniel sees two images of the same reality — one near and one far — through the lens of biblical prophecy. Much like our own lives, where present circumstances and future plans are woven together, Daniel's vision reminds us of the intricate interplay between history and God's divine purpose.

As we navigate the complexities of our lives, it's easy to feel as if we're experiencing double vision — seeing the challenges of today and the uncertainties of tomorrow. But just as a pair of corrective lenses brings clarity to our physical sight, faith functions as the spiritual corrective lens for our souls.

The Apostle Paul encourages us in 2 Corinthians 5:7, "For we walk by faith, not by sight." Faith allows us to see beyond the immediate circumstances, recognizing that God is at work in our present, preparing us for His future plans. It is through the lens of faith that we discern the purpose behind our trials and triumphs.

So, let us embrace the divine prescription of faith, trusting that God's vision for our lives extends beyond what we can currently perceive. As we face the challenges of today, may we walk by faith, knowing that God is guiding us through the lens of His eternal plan, bringing clarity to our journey and hope to our hearts.

Day 54

TREASURE HUNT

"I, Daniel, understood by the books the number of the years specified by the word of the Lord through Jeremiah the prophet, that He would accomplish seventy years in the desolations of Jerusalem."

DANIEL 9:2

IN the world of treasure hunting, seasoned adventurers embark on epic journeys armed with ancient maps, cryptic clues, and a relentless determination to uncover hidden riches. These intrepid seekers know that the pursuit of treasure demands patience, perseverance, and a steadfast commitment to the promise of discovery.

There are valuable truths to be discovered in the treasure trove of Scripture.

Likewise, in the spiritual realm, Daniel diligently studied the Scriptures, comparing past revelations to discern the unfolding mysteries of God's plan. His journey begins by reading Jeremiah's prophecy containing clues pointing to a grand promise — a promise of deliverance for the nation of Israel from their 70-year exile in Babylon (Jeremiah 29:10). Daniel, like a skillful treasure hunter, understands that there are valuable truths to be discovered in the treasure trove of Scripture.

Fueled by curiosity and a hunger for God's wisdom, Daniel takes his findings to the Lord in prayer. His heart, like the treasure hunter's, beats with anticipation as he seeks further insight and understanding. In the solitude of prayer, Daniel lays before God the map he has discovered in the ancient scrolls, pleading for guidance in the journey ahead.

The psalmist, in Psalm 19:10, declares, "God's precepts are more to be desired than gold, Yea, than much fine gold; Sweeter also than honey and the honeycomb." This sentiment captures the essence of Daniel's attitude towards the Scriptures. The promises of God are more precious than the finest gold, and the wisdom contained within them is sweeter than honey.

As we follow in Daniel's footsteps, embracing the role of treasure hunters in the vast expanse of God's Word, we realize that there are countless profound truths to be uncovered. God's Word serves as an accurate map leading us to the valuable treasures of truth, wisdom, and guidance for our lives.

This journey, like any grand quest for treasure, demands diligence, patience, and perseverance. The pursuit of God's wisdom is not a fleeting endeavor, but a life-long commitment that brings exhilaration and fulfillment. Just as Daniel's faithfulness was rewarded with the unfolding of God's plan, so too can our persistence and dedication lead us to the discovery of invaluable treasures hidden in the sacred pages of Scripture.

In light of this hope, let us approach the Word of God with the heart of a treasure hunter, understanding that there are priceless truths waiting to be unearthed. With each turn of the page, let us embark on a thrilling adventure, knowing that in our pursuit of God's wisdom, we will discover the grandest treasure of all — a deeper and richer relationship with the Almighty.

Day 55

A MIRROR REFLECTION

> "Then I set my face toward the Lord God to make request by prayer and supplications, with fasting, sackcloth, and ashes. And I prayed to the Lord my God, and made confession."
>
> **DANIEL 9:3-4**

IMAGINE walking through a carnival and stumbling upon a distorted mirror — those funhouse mirrors that warp your reflection into exaggerated shapes and sizes. Your once familiar image becomes stretched and twisted, leaving you barely recognizable. It's all in good fun, but there's a powerful analogy hidden in the distortion of that reflection.

In Daniel 9:3-4, we find Daniel, not at a carnival, but in the depths of his soul, seeking God with an urgency, humility, and brokenness that mirrors the sincere heart of a repentant believer. Daniel's prayer of confession serves as a profound reflection, much like the image we see in a mirror, but in this case, it's a mirror of God's holiness and righteousness.

Just as a carnival mirror distorts our appearance, sin distorts our spiritual reflection in the mirror of God's purity. The clearer we visualize the image of God's purity, the more accurately we see the reflection of our iniquity. Like Daniel, we are called to confront the distorted and blemished nature of our souls.

Daniel, deeply grieved with godly sorrow over his sin and the sin of his people Israel, urgently sought God through prayer and fasting. His confession wasn't a casual acknowledgment of wrongdoing; it was a thorough and specific admission of failure and flaws before a holy God. Daniel recognized the disparity between God's righteousness and his own shortcomings, and he approached God with a humble heart, seeking forgiveness, grace, and mercy.

In the same way, when we stand before the mirror of God's righteousness, we may see a reflection marred by our sins. Yet, there is hope. The Scriptures assures us in 1 John 1:9 that "If we confess our sins, God is faithful and just to forgive us our sins and to cleanse us from all unrighteousness." This promise is our invitation to approach God with the brokenness, humility, and confession that Daniel exemplified.

The clearer we visualize the image of God's purity, the more accurately we see the reflection of our iniquity.

As we bring our distorted and blemished reflections to our Heavenly Father, He responds with merciful grace. God's forgiveness and cleansing restores our marred image into a reflection of Christ's righteousness in us. The carnival mirror may entertain, but the mirror of God's holiness transforms. Let us, like Daniel, approach this mirror with sincerity, allowing God to reshape us into reflections of His glory.

Day 56

EVERY LITTLE DETAIL

"Now therefore, our God, hear the prayer of Your servant, and his supplications, and for the Lord's sake, cause Your face to shine on Your sanctuary, which is desolate."

DANIEL 9:17

HAVE you ever purchased a piece of furniture that required assembly? If so, you understand the importance of following every little detail in the instructions. Skipping a step or neglecting a piece could result in an unsafe or dysfunctional final product. In the same way, our spiritual lives require attention to detail, particularly when it comes to prayer.

Daniel, a man known for his righteousness, found himself overwhelmed by the weight of his iniquity and disobedience when he considered the righteousness and faithfulness of God. In Daniel 9:17, we see him earnestly praying, acknowledging his transgressions, and appealing to God's mercy. Daniel understood that to approach God with sincerity, he needed to be specific about the details of his repentance.

In the midst of confessing his sins, Daniel focused his supplications on the restoration of God's city, Jerusalem, His sanctuary, and His people. His prayer was not vague; instead, it was filled with specific details. Daniel understood the importance of addressing every aspect of his life before God, just like assembling each piece of furniture meticulously.

Likewise, our prayers should not be vague or half-hearted. God invites us to come to Him with the specifics of our needs, concerns, and desires. Philippians 4:6 encourages us, "Be anxious for nothing, but in everything by prayer and supplication, with thanksgiving, let your requests be made known to God." There is no detail too small for God to consider. He cares about every aspect of our lives.

When we find ourselves overwhelmed with worry and anxiety, we can turn to God in prayer, laying out all the unpleasant details before Him. Just as in assembling furniture, where we trust that every detail matters, in prayer, we can trust that God is intimately concerned about the intricate details of our lives. This promise assures us that as we lay down our burdens before Him in prayer, He is faithful to pick them up.

God is intimately concerned about the intricate details of our lives.

The next time you're tempted to skip prayer or seek alternative solutions to life's challenges, remember that God cares about even the little details of your life. Approach Him with sincerity, confessing your sins, and presenting your specific needs. God, the Master Assembler, hears your prayers and desires to guide you in assembling a life that honors and glorifies Him. So, let every detail of your life be laid before the One who cares for you deeply. Trust in His faithfulness, for in prayer, every little detail matters.

Day 57

GOD KNOWS OUR NEEDS

"While I was speaking in prayer, Gabriel, whom I had seen in the vision at the beginning, being caused to fly swiftly, reached me at the time of the evening offering."

DANIEL 9:21

I N today's fast-paced world, it's hard to imagine life without the convenience of Wi-Fi. We are accustomed to being connected, seamlessly and wirelessly, to a vast world of information. Just as Wi-Fi signals invisibly surround us, connecting us to limitless unseen data, so does our connection with God through prayer. In the book of Daniel, we witness a powerful example of this divine connection.

Prayer is not meant to inform God but transform us.

Daniel, during a time of confession and supplication, experienced a remarkable moment. In the midst of pouring out his heart to God, the angel Gabriel swiftly responded to his petitions even before he had finished speaking. Imagine the immediate and direct response from God, mirroring the way Wi-Fi instantly connects us to the digital world.

This interaction reveals a profound truth about our communication with God. Daniel's experience echoes the words of Jesus in the New Testament, reminding us that our Heavenly Father knows our needs even before we give

Him our pleads. In Matthew 6:8, Jesus says, "For your Father knows the things you have need of before you ask Him." This divine knowledge demonstrates a level of intimacy and care that surpasses our understanding.

Consider the marvel of being heard and answered by God, while we are still in the act of praying. It's a reflection of God's constant awareness of our deepest desires and concerns. Our connection with God is not hindered by physical barriers or limited by time and space. The Lord, in His omniscience, comprehends our needs before we present them to Him.

This reality reminds us that prayer is not meant to inform God but transform us. Prayers are not merely a list of requests for God to consider; they are a means of transforming our hearts, aligning our will with His, and deepening our relationship with the Creator. God's immediate response to Daniel underscores the personal and attentive nature of our Heavenly Father.

Just as Wi-Fi enables us to access information effortlessly, our prayers provide a direct line of communication with God, allowing us to receive His compassion, provision, and guidance. God's love for us transcends our understanding, and He desires to meet our needs even before we ask. Therefore, let us approach the throne of grace with confidence, knowing that our prayers are heard, and our Heavenly Father is intimately acquainted with the cries of our hearts.

Day 58
GREATLY LOVED BY GOD

> "At the beginning of your supplications the command went out, and I have come to tell you, for you are greatly beloved; therefore consider the matter, and understand the vision."
>
> **DANIEL 9:23**

IN the tender embrace of a loving parent, a child finds solace and security. A parent's heart is intricately woven with threads of unconditional love, a love that seeks the well-being and safety of the child above all else. Just as a devoted parent anticipates and meets the needs of their beloved child, so too does our Heavenly Father shower us with immeasurable love.

Imagine the watchful eyes of a parent observing their child's every move, discerning their unspoken worries and understanding their deepest desires. It is a love that transcends mere sentiment; it is a love that compels action. In the same way, God's love for us moves Him to action, attending to our prayers and concerns with a depth of care beyond our comprehension.

In the quiet moments of prayer, Daniel sought God's wisdom and guidance in the midst of uncertainty. As he poured out his heart in supplication, God responded with a message of profound reassurance through the angel: "For you are greatly beloved." Consider the weight of those words, echoing the sentiments of a parent whispering to a cherished child, "You are greatly loved."

Picture the relief flooding Daniel's soul as he realized that God had heard his prayers, sent an answer, and affirmed his beloved status. In times of distress, God's love breaks through the trials of life and calms our hearts with His peace.

1 John 3:1 declares, "Behold what manner of love the Father has bestowed on us, that we should be called children of God!" God's love is not a distant, passive sentiment. It is an active, intentional love that responds to our needs and desires. It is a love that transcends the storms of life, providing comfort and assurance.

God's love has a way of settling our nerves when the storms of life are near. Just as the presence of a parent brings comfort to a frightened child, knowing that everything will be alright, we can find solace in the unfailing love of our Heavenly Father. His love is not confined to mere words but is demonstrated through His constant vigilance over our lives.

God's love has a way of settling our nerves when the storms of life are near.

Today, trust in the depth of God's love, knowing that, like a caring parent, He always has His eyes on you. In moments of fear or doubt, take refuge in the truth that you are greatly loved by God, and His love is a beacon of light that dispels the darkness, bringing peace and assurance to your soul.

Day 59

PROPHETIC ITINERARY

"Seventy weeks are determined for your people and your holy city, to finish the transgression, to make an end of sins, to make reconciliation for iniquity, to bring in everlasting righteousness, to seal up vision and prophecy, and to anoint the Most Holy."

DANIEL 9:24

IN the busyness of our daily lives, planning a vacation can be a daunting task. The stress of coordinating flights, booking accommodations, and organizing transportation can take away from the joy of anticipating a well-deserved break. This is where a travel agent becomes invaluable, meticulously organizing an itinerary with specific details to ensure a seamless and enjoyable experience for the traveler.

Imagine if God were our divine travel agent, guiding us through the intricacies of His prophetic itinerary.

✷
God's prophetic itinerary is a futuristic certainty.

In the book of Daniel, we are granted a glimpse into God's meticulous plan for the future of Israel. Just as a travel agent plans every detail of a journey, God has carefully organized a prophetic itinerary that unfolds over a specific period of time.

God reveals to Daniel a timeframe — 70 weeks, equivalent to 490 years — divided into three distinct sections. The first segment focuses on the rebuilding of Jerusalem, the second on the arrival of the Messiah, and the third on future events during the great tribulation.

Just as a travel agent ensures clients arrive at their destinations on a predetermined date and time, God has orchestrated specific events in His prophetic itinerary. The triumphal entry of Jesus into Jerusalem, as foretold in the vision, marked a pivotal moment in God's plan. Luke 19:42 captures the significance of "this day" when Jesus identifies the prophetic fulfillment of the arrival of God's peace.

Based on these fulfillments, God's prophetic itinerary is a futuristic certainty. The divine plan encompasses the culmination of God's redemptive design through the sacrifice of Jesus on the cross for sinful humanity. Every detail has been carefully arranged to put an end to sin, transgression, and to bring in everlasting righteousness.

Just as a travel agent explains to clients what to expect on their upcoming trip, God has provided us with details regarding what is certain as His prophetic itinerary unfolds. The journey includes the ultimate destination: the triumph of Jesus over sin and death, bringing peace to a world in need.

In the grand scheme of God's plan, we find assurance and hope. As we trust in His prophetic itinerary, we anticipate the culmination of His redemptive work. The sacrifice of Jesus on the cross is the centerpiece of this divine journey, providing a way for humanity to experience everlasting righteousness. Don't miss the trip of a lifetime — God's prophetic itinerary is unfolding, and the destination is the fulfillment of His promise to reconcile, redeem, and bring eternal peace.

Day 60

A PROPHETIC PAUSE

"And after sixty-two weeks Messiah shall be cut off, but not for Himself."

DANIEL 9:26A

IN the fast-paced world of sports, especially in critical moments of a game, teams often call for a huddle or timeout. These brief breaks from the action allow players to regroup, refocus, and receive strategic instructions from their coach. The purpose is clear — to unify the team around carefully planned plays that will hopefully lead to victory. Interestingly, in the grand game of prophecy, Daniel's vision introduces us to a similar concept — a prophetic pause with a purpose.

Daniel's 70-week vision, a meticulous countdown of years, reveals two monumental events that have already transpired: the rebuilding of Jerusalem under Nehemiah's leadership and the arrival of Jesus Christ as the sacrificial Messiah. However, the vision also unveils a future event — the rise of the Antichrist during the great tribulation. Between these pivotal moments, there exists a prophetic timeout — a divine pause in which we presently live.

During God's prophetic timeout, He has given the church a purposeful game plan. After Christ's resurrection, He commissioned the church to preach the gospel and make disciples of all nations (Matthew 28:19-20). This divine directive is rooted in God's patience and desire for all to come to salvation (2 Peter 3:9). He orchestrates a divine timeout so that the gospel may be proclaimed, hearts may turn to Him, and His redemptive purposes may be fulfilled.

In this holy huddle, believers are invited to focus on God's purpose and plans. As the play clock of Daniel's prophecy is momentarily stopped, we are called to renew our sense of urgency, to run with endurance the race set before us (Hebrews 12:1). The divine coach encourages us to serve others with His love and compassion until the prophetic clock starts again with the imminent return of Jesus.

During God's prophetic timeout, He has given the church a purposeful game plan.

This prophetic pause is not a time for complacency, but a call to action. God invites us into His huddle, not to sit idly but to receive His strategy and then, with a renewed sense of purpose, to jump right back into the game of life. The mission is clear: share the gospel, make disciples, and advance the kingdom until the prophetic clock resumes its countdown.

As we stand in the midst of God's prophetic pause, let us heed the divine coach's call. Embrace the purpose He has entrusted to the church, and with a sense of urgency born out of His love, run the race before us. The prophetic timeout is a gracious interlude — an invitation to align our lives with God's eternal game plan, to share the gospel with passion, and to eagerly anticipate the day when the prophetic clock resumes with the triumphant return of our Lord and Savior, Jesus Christ.

Day 61

A SORROWFUL HEART

"In those days, I, Daniel, was mourning three full weeks."

DANIEL 10:2

IN the aftermath of natural disasters, we witness a profound outpouring of compassion. Television screens showcase heartbreaking scenes of devastation, leaving us moved with empathy for those affected. We see families torn apart, homes reduced to rubble, and communities grappling with the weight of loss. In response to this shared sorrow, something extraordinary happens — the human heart is stirred to action.

Just as many respond to the cries of the suffering by opening their hearts and wallets, the prophet Daniel too experienced a deep stirring within him. His people, Israel, were facing a future marked by suffering and distress. This burden weighed heavily on Daniel's heart, much like the heavy burdens that afflict people in the wake of personal disasters and grief today.

Daniel's reaction was not one of indifference or resignation. He was not content to simply acknowledge the suffering from a distance. Instead, he chose to respond with a heart moved with compassion that led him to seek God persistently through fasting and intercessory prayer for three full weeks. Daniel's anguish and his earnest seeking of God's intervention exemplify a profound truth: in the face of suffering, a compassionate heart seeks divine intervention.

In our lives, we encounter individuals facing personal disasters of mourning, grief, and sorrow. The call to action for us is similar to the compassionate response we witness in times of natural disasters. It is an invitation to bear the burdens of others as though they were our own. The Scriptures beckon us to cultivate a heart that is tender, compassionate, and empathetic. 2 Corinthians 1:3-4 speaks of the tremendous extent of God's comfort to soothe our sorrowful hearts.

God's comfort flows through you in bringing relief to those bearing grief.

This verse also reminds us that God's comfort is not reserved solely for our benefit. Rather, it is bestowed upon us so that we, in turn, may become vessels of that comfort to others. God's comfort flows through you in bringing relief to those bearing grief. When we see someone weighed down by the burdens of life, we are called to be the hands and feet of God's compassion.

Just as people generously give to relief organizations in times of disaster, we are encouraged to generously give of ourselves in times of personal distress. Whether it be through a listening ear, a helping hand, or a prayer offered on behalf of the hurting, we have the opportunity to bring God's comfort and relief to those in need.

In cultivating a compassionate heart, we emulate the very character of God. As we respond to the sorrows around us, let us remember the example of Daniel, who, moved with deep compassion, sought God persistently on behalf of his people. Likewise, may we be catalysts for change, messengers of God's comfort, and relief in a world that desperately needs it.

Day 62

WAITING ON GOD

"Do not fear, Daniel, for from the first day that you set your heart to understand, and to humble yourself before your God, your words were heard."

DANIEL 10:12

WE often hear the saying, "Good things come to those who wait." This adage encourages us to embrace patience and diligence, assuring us that in due time, our efforts will be rewarded with positive outcomes. This principle, though often applied to various aspects of life, finds resonance in the spiritual realm as well. The story of Daniel exemplifies the significance of waiting on God and the profound lessons that can be gleaned in the process.

Sometimes a delay in answered prayer is intended to develop a deeper dependency on God.

Daniel provides us with a powerful example of persistence in prayer. On one specific occasion, Daniel set his heart to seek God's understanding. However, unlike previous instances where God's response was swift, this time, Daniel found himself in a three-week period of fervent prayer and waiting.

Daniel learned that waiting on God is never wasted time. He understood that sometimes, the delay in God's response is part of a divine plan. Similarly, in our lives, we may experience delays in answered prayers. It is crucial to recognize that God's timing is purposeful and sovereign. Ultimately, delays in answered prayer develops a deeper dependency on God.

Remarkably, in heaven, our prayers matter and move God. Daniel's perseverance in prayer resulted in a powerful revelation. An angel came to comfort him, assuring Daniel that from the very first day he prayed, his words were heard. However, there was a delay in the response due to spiritual battles unfolding beyond his sight.

This truth is a comforting reminder for us. Our prayers are not in vain. They reach the ears of God, and He responds, even if the answer is not immediate. So, don't stop praying because any delays in answered prayer may be an opportunity for God to work in unseen ways, aligning circumstances for a more significant impact.

Isaiah 40:31 encourages us with a similar promise: "But those who wait on the Lord shall renew their strength; they shall mount up with wings like eagles, they shall run and not be weary, they shall walk and not faint." God assures us that in seasons of waiting, He is actively working to strengthen us.

Daniel's life teaches us that waiting on God is an essential aspect of our spiritual journey. While delays may test our patience, they are an opportunity for God to shape us, strengthen us, and prepare us for the blessings He has in store. So, let us press into prayer, understanding that even in the waiting, God is at work. May we not lose heart, for in His perfect timing, the breakthrough will come, bringing with it the fulfillment of His promises.

Day 63

SPIRITUAL HOSTILITY

"But the prince of the Persian kingdom resisted me twenty-one days. Then Michael, one of the chief princes, came to help me."

DANIEL 10:13

IN the digital age, our computers and mobile devices are constantly under the threat of spyware — malicious software that stealthily infiltrates our systems, tracks our activities, and sends our personal data to third parties without our knowledge or consent. Recent statistics reveal that a staggering 90% of U.S. home computers have fallen victim to spyware infections at some point. To protect against these hidden threats, we install antivirus software that acts as a vigilant guardian, scanning network data and blocking the infiltration of dangerous spyware.

Just as our digital world faces unseen threats, so too does our spiritual realm. In the book of Daniel, we catch a glimpse of the spiritual battles that rage behind the scenes, hindering the prayers of God's people. Daniel 10:13 introduces us to a formidable adversary — the prince of the Persian kingdom, an evil angelic being that resisted the angel sent to answer Daniel's prayers.

Ephesians 6:12 reminds us that our struggle is not against flesh and blood but against the spiritual forces of evil. The battles we face are often the result of spiritual warfare unleashed upon us by demonic principalities, powers, and dominions. Like spyware silently invading our devices, these spiritual adversaries seek to undermine God's purposes and plans. Jesus Himself referred to Satan as the prince of the world, highlighting the adversary's role in engaging in spiritual warfare to influence generations and nations against God. The parallels between the digital and spiritual realms are striking. Both involve unseen forces working tirelessly to gain access, track activities, and disrupt the proper functioning of the system.

In the realm of spiritual warfare, demonic hostility is a battlefield certainty for God's divine infantry — believers in Christ. Just as our computers are under constant threat, so are we. The prince of the air, Satan, seeks to hinder our prayers, distort our perceptions, and sow discord among God's people.

Yet, the good news is that we are not defenseless. Just as we install antivirus software to protect our devices, God equips us with the armor of God (Ephesians 6:13-18) to stand firm in the face of spiritual battles. This divine armor acts as our spiritual antivirus, blocking and protecting against the hidden threats of the enemy.

Demonic hostility is a battlefield certainty for God's divine infantry.

As followers of Christ, we must recognize the reality of spiritual warfare. The prince of the world may seek to hinder our prayers, but we are assured of victory through the power of God. Let us stand firm in the armor of God, extinguishing the fiery darts of the enemy and guarding against constant attacks. In the unseen battles of the spiritual realm, may we remain vigilant, knowing that our ultimate security lies in the protection of the Almighty.

Day 64

CLEANSE MY SPEECH

"One having the likeness of the sons of men touched my lips, then I opened my mouth and spoke."

DANIEL 10:16

As children, many of us were taught the saying, "Sticks and stones may break my bones, but words will never hurt me." It was a shield against the verbal arrows of bullying and name-calling, an attempt to fortify our tender hearts against the harsh realities of life. Little did we know that as we matured, we would come to understand the profound truth that our words possess a power far beyond what we could have imagined in our youth.

> ✱
> *Often what flows into our hearts eventually falls off of our lips.*

In the book of Daniel, we find a powerful illustration of the impact of purified speech. When Daniel encountered the Divine, he fell to the ground, trembling in fear before the majesty of God. In that awe-inspiring moment, one with the likeness of the sons of men touched his lips, purifying his speech. It's a vivid reminder that our words take on a sacred significance in the presence of the holy.

Isaiah also experienced a similar revelation. In Isaiah 6:5, when confronted with the holiness of God, he recognized the filthiness of sin saying, "Woe is me for I am a man of unclean lips." His honest confession led to purification, a transformation initiated by God Himself. Our tongues, like Isaiah's, are challenging to tame, and often what flows into our hearts eventually falls off of our lips.

That is why Scripture repeatedly emphasizes the importance of guarding our speech. Ephesians 4:29 admonishes us, "Let no corrupt word proceed out of your mouth, but what is good for necessary edification, that it may impart grace to the hearers." Our words should not be sources of corruption but instruments of edification, imparting grace to those around us.

It's also crucial to recognize that the words we speak have a lasting impact, shaping the lives and hearts of those who hear them. Proverbs 18:21 declares, "Death and life are in the power of the tongue." Our speech has the potential to breathe life into weary souls or inflict wounds that may take years to heal.

Just as Daniel and Isaiah sought purification in the presence of God, we too, must allow our speech to be cleansed. When we stand before the Almighty, it's a humbling experience, acknowledging our inadequacy and seeking His transformative touch on our words. God's desire is not to stifle our expression but to refine it, aligning our speech with the holiness and grace that characterize His nature.

Let us, therefore, be intentional about the words we choose. May our speech reflect the purity that comes from communion with God. As we allow Him to purify our hearts, our words will naturally follow suit, becoming instruments of grace, encouragement, and love. By fulfilling this exhortation our tongues become a fountain of life, bringing healing and blessing to those around us.

Day 65

WEAK MADE STRONG

"As for me, no strength remains in me now, nor is any breath left in me. Then again, the one having the likeness of a man touched me and strengthened me."

DANIEL 10:17-18

IN the ancient Japanese art form of Kintsugi, broken pottery is not discarded; instead, it is meticulously repaired using a special lacquer mixed with powdered gold, silver, or platinum. This process highlights the cracks and fractures, turning the brokenness into a thing of beauty. The result is a piece of art that celebrates the history and imperfections of the vessel, making it more valuable than before.

In Daniel 10:17-18, we find the prophet Daniel overwhelmed by a glorious vision. His encounter left him weak, frail, and filled with fear. The brilliance of the vision had sapped his strength, and he found himself unable to stand. It is in this moment of vulnerability that God intervenes, sending a touch that not only strengthens Daniel but also eases his fear.

Similarly, God uses our weaknesses as opportunities to showcase His strength, turning moments of fragility into demonstrations of His glory. The best way to demonstrate God's strength is to celebrate our weakness. Much like the art of Kintsugi, God takes our broken pieces and, instead of hiding them, adorns them with His strength. Our weaknesses become an incredible testimony, showcasing God's transformative power in our lives.

This paradoxical truth is evident not only in Daniel's experience, but also in the life of the Apostle Paul. In 2 Corinthians 12:9, Paul recounts his own plea for relief from a major weakness. God's response was, "My grace is sufficient for you, for My strength is made perfect in weakness." Paul realized that God's strength was most evident when he acknowledged his own weakness. In the broken places of our lives, God's strength is made perfect, shining forth as a testament to His glory.

The best way to demonstrate God's strength is to celebrate our weakness.

Just as Kintsugi highlights the brokenness of pottery, we are called to celebrate our weaknesses. When God touches our brokenness, His strength becomes the golden lacquer that not only mends, but also enhances our value. Our broken history, when mended by God's hands, becomes a story of redemption, restoration, and transformation. Our weaknesses, like the golden seams in Kintsugi, draw attention not to our frailty but to the radiant glory of God at work within us.

As vessels of clay, we are all subject to cracks and fractures. Yet, in the hands of the divine potter, our brokenness is transformed into an image of God's strength and glory. Let us not hide our weaknesses but celebrate them, for in doing so, we showcase the beauty of God's restoration. Like Daniel, may we be touched and strengthened in our moments of weakness, becoming living testimonies to the power of God's grace. As we embrace our frailties, may others be drawn not to our perfection, but to the magnificent beauty of the God who repairs and restores.

Day 66

FEAR NOT

"He said, 'O man greatly beloved, fear not! Peace be to you; be strong, yes, be strong!' So when he spoke to me, I was strengthened."

DANIEL 10:19

IN the depths of the Great Depression, Franklin D. Roosevelt assumed the presidency of the United States. The nation was gripped with fear and uncertainty about the future. In his inaugural address, Roosevelt uttered timeless words that echo through history, "the only thing we have to fear is fear itself." The anticipation surrounding his speech mirrored the anxiety of the people, much like the apprehension that enveloped Daniel as he faced visions of impending trials and hardships.

Roosevelt's words were a beacon of hope, much like the angel's comforting message to Daniel. In times of fear, words have the power to uplift and strengthen, guiding us through the darkness of uncertainty. Most of the things we obsessively worry about never actually come about, yet fear has a way of creeping into our hearts and minds, causing worry and anxiety.

Roosevelt's inaugural speech was poignant because he identified that fear causes us to see life through a filter of worry. Fear is an emotion easily overcome when we understand that it is a negative force drawing our attention away from reality. Similarly, when Daniel looked at the circumstances around him, he was filled with fear and worry. However, God

Spoke through the angel, redirecting his focus onto the sovereignty of God, who is in control and is an ever-present help in time of need.

In Joshua 1:9, we find a leader, Joshua, timid and fearful as he assumed leadership in Israel. God addressed his concerns as well, reminding him that fear has no place in our hearts when God is at the center of our lives. In the face of overwhelming obstacles and crippling fear, God would say the same to us: "Be strong and of good courage; do not be afraid, nor be dismayed, for the Lord your God is with you wherever you go."

The words "fear not" resonate not only as a command, but also as an invitation to experience a transformative power beyond fear. Just as the angel's message fortified Daniel to face his trials, we too, can draw strength from this promise. It is a power that transcends circumstances and dispels the shadows of anxiety. This power is rooted in the understanding that God's love and sovereignty eclipse the grip of fear. Embracing this truth allows us to navigate life with a spirit of resilience and hope.

Most of the things we obsessively worry about never actually come about.

In moments of fear and uncertainty, remember that you are greatly beloved by God. He fills us with courage, and promises His abiding presence in the midst of worry and fear. Just as Roosevelt's words brought hope to a nation in despair, God's words to us are a source of strength and peace. Fear not, for God is with you, and His perfect love casts out all fear. Be strong, yes, be strong, and let your heart take courage, for the Lord is with you.

Day 67
SCRIPTURES OF TRUTH

"But I will tell you what is noted in the Scripture of Truth."

DANIEL 10:21

IN the quest for truth, humanity has devised various methods to discern honesty from deception. One such method is the polygraph, commonly known as a lie detector test. This device, monitoring physiological responses, aims to identify deceptive answers by detecting variations in indicators such as blood pressure, pulse, and respiration. While it is not foolproof, its accuracy, when conducted correctly, suggests a profound connection between physiological responses and truthfulness.

There is no greater detector of truth than the revelation found in the Scripture of Truth.

In Daniel 10:21, we encounter a fascinating revelation about a different kind of truth detector — the "Scripture of Truth." This Scripture, not subject to the limitations of human devices, stands as an infallible testimony to the absolute truth. It is a divine polygraph that transcends the boundaries of time, offering insights into the past, present, and future. Like a lie detector reveals deception, the Scripture of Truth unveils the eternal truths of God.

Daniel, a prophet granted remarkable insights into future events, faced opposition from evil spiritual forces seeking to distort God's plans and mislead humanity. The struggle Daniel encountered echoes the ongoing battle between truth and deception in our lives. However, the assurance given to Daniel is our assurance as well — a promise that nothing can thwart or deceptively twist the will of God as revealed in Scripture.

Psalm 119:160 emphatically declares, "The entirety of Your Word is truth, and every one of Your righteous judgments endures forever." The psalmist's declaration affirms the sentiment that every word in the Scripture of Truth is absolute and enduring truth. Unlike the fallibility of human expressions, God's Word stands steadfast, unchanging, and eternal. It is a foundation upon which we can confidently build our lives.

Proverbs 30:5 adds, "Every word of God is pure; He is a shield to those who put their trust in Him." Just as a lie detector test assesses the purity of one's responses, God's Word passes every truth test. It is pure, untainted by the deceptions that plague our world. As we encounter uncertainties, God's Word serves as an unwavering guide, a shield protecting those who trust in its veracity.

In a world that constantly challenges and questions truth, let us remember that there is no greater detector of truth than the revelation found in the Scripture of Truth. The complete accuracy and enduring legacy of God's Word provides us with the confidence to trust in the infallible nature of His promises. Let us anchor our faith in God's Word that stands the test of time for His promises are sure, His truth is undeniable, and His purposes will prevail.

Day 68

SPOILER ALERT

"He shall do according to his own will, and no one shall stand against him. He shall stand in the Glorious Land with destruction in his power."

DANIEL 11:16

WHEN it comes to movies and books, the term "spoiler alert" has become a familiar caution, signaling readers or viewers that what follows contains crucial details that could reveal significant elements of the story. Just as we appreciate these warnings to preserve the thrill of experiencing a narrative for the first time, the Bible, too, contains spoiler alerts of a different kind — divine revelations about the unfolding drama of human history.

As God's people, knowing the end of the story we can live in the present with full confidence in the Lord.

The verse from Daniel 11:16 places us in the midst of geopolitical intrigue, where powerful leaders stand in the Glorious Land with the potential for destruction in their power. This setting unfolds over a period of 375 years, spanning the conflicts between the Persian and Greek Empires, with a particular focus on the struggles between Syrian and Egyptian kings. The geographical location of Israel in the Middle East places God's people directly between warring nations —

reminding us that followers of God are often caught in the crossfire of world powers.

Much like a meticulous movie or book review, the prophetic words to Daniel disclose complex details about historical events. The intricate narrative covers centuries of human history, unveiling the rise and fall of empires, wars, and the struggles of nations. As we read, we're reminded that God is not only the ultimate critic, but also the sovereign director of history.

Isaiah 46:10 reiterates this point, declaring, "I make known the end from the beginning, from ancient times, what is still to come. I say, 'My purpose will stand, and I will do all that I please.'" God, through the Scriptures, provides the ultimate historical spoiler alert, offering us insights into the plots of humanity and the divine purposes that will be fulfilled. The events described in Daniel are not merely a recounting of history, but a revelation of God's ongoing work in orchestrating His redemptive plan.

Just as God predicted the rise and fall of powerful kingdoms with precision in the past, He has also provided us with the final future spoiler alert — the victory of God over sin and the promised return of Jesus. Armed with the assurance of the ultimate triumph of good over evil, we can navigate the present with confidence.

As we journey through the pages of prophecy and history, we find comfort in the divine spoiler alerts that assure us of God's sovereignty over the tumultuous events of the world. Through the intricate details of Scripture, we get a glimpse of the unfolding drama of redemption and restoration. Let us live in the present with complete confidence, knowing that the Lord holds the future, and has already declared the final chapters of the story.

Day 69

GODLY PROMOTIONS

"In his place shall arise a vile person, to whom they will not give the honor of royalty; but he shall come peaceably, seizing the kingdom by intrigue."

DANIEL 11:21

IN competitive sports, few stories captivate the world as much as Lance Armstrong's meteoric rise and subsequent fall. From 1999 to 2005, Armstrong astounded the cycling world by winning seven consecutive Tour de France titles and an Olympic medal after overcoming a battle with cancer. His triumphs were celebrated as a testament to the human spirit's resilience and determination.

However, as time unfolded, a dark truth emerged. Lance Armstrong's victories, which had seemed like the epitome of hard work and dedication, were tarnished by the revelation of his use of performance-enhancing drugs. His ascent to the pinnacle of cycling glory was not a result of pure athleticism, but rather a deceptive journey marked by cheating and dishonesty.

In Daniel's vision, we encounter a similar narrative of deceitful tactics used to capture power, authority, and control. The rise of one such leader, not the rightful successor to the throne by royal lineage, is foretold. This individual employs deception, trickery, and flattery to assume power, much like Armstrong's manipulation of the cycling world.

Sadly, such maneuvers are not confined to the world of sports or ancient visions. In the pursuit of success and promotion, the world often values cunning and manipulation over integrity and hard work. This can result in dishonest means that cheat others out of well-deserved positions, mirroring the deception seen in Armstrong's scandal.

As Christians, we are called to a higher standard. The Bible encourages us to act with integrity, honesty, and diligence in all aspects of our lives. In so doing, we recognize that our actions should seek to glorify God alone. Psalm 75:6-7 reassures us, "For exaltation comes neither from the east nor from the west nor from the south. But God is the Judge: He puts down one, and exalts another."

Godly advancements are the only worldly achievements that ever truly matter.

Our promotion and success should not come from manipulating circumstances or using deceitful tactics, but from living a life that pleases and honors God. Thus, godly advancements are the only worldly achievements that ever truly matter. By remaining faithful to God with Christ-like character in both our public and private lives, we can trust that God will bring about the proper promotions and rewards in His perfect timing and appropriate way.

In a world that often rewards deceit, let us be a people who stand firm in our commitment to honesty and integrity. Instead of relying on manipulative strategies for advancement, let us trust in God as the ultimate facilitator of our success. In doing so, we participate in a higher narrative of godly promotions, where the rewards are lasting and the honor is eternal.

Day 70
EVIL ENTICEMENTS

"Both these kings' hearts shall be bent on evil,
and they shall speak lies at the same table;
but it shall not prosper."

DANIEL 11:27

IN the dark and mysterious depths of the ocean, the anglerfish lurks, a master of cunning and deception. With a bioluminescent lure hanging in front of its mouth, this deep-sea predator entices unsuspecting prey into its deadly trap. The allure of the glowing bait, resembling a small, harmless organism, draws curious fish closer, unaware of the peril that awaits them.

While Satan seeks to ensnare us with evil inventions, God, in His infinite grace, assures us of His good intentions.

In Daniel 11:27, we encounter a warning about the hidden motives and evil intentions of future kings. This verse paints a picture of hearts bent on evil, weaving lies in the shadows of their deceit. Much like the anglerfish, these rulers create alluring enticements to lure others into precarious situations they never saw coming.

The anglerfish's hunting strategy serves as an analogy for the evil intentions that characterize the actions of these kings. Their deceptive maneuvers and cunning words also mirror the sinister tactics of our spiritual adversary, Satan. Like the anglerfish, Satan employs the art of enticement, weaving lies and promises of fulfillment to draw us into a trap of destruction.

The Bible describes Satan as the father of lies (John 8:44), emphasizing his role in deceiving humanity. He prowls like a roaring lion, seeking whom he may devour (1 Peter 5:8). His enticing tactics may seem attractive, promising pleasure and satisfaction, but behind the façade lies a sinister agenda to steal, kill, and destroy (John 10:10).

Romans 8:28 provides a stark contrast to the deceitful tactics of the evil one, declaring, "And we know that all things work together for good to those that love God, to those who are called according to His purpose." This verse reminds us that God is at work for our good, even in the face of the enticements and schemes of the enemy. While Satan seeks to ensnare us with evil inventions, God, in His infinite grace, assures us of His good intentions.

As believers, we must be vigilant, recognizing the alluring traps of the enemy. Satan will lie to our faces, accusing us behind our backs, all with the aim of cutting our knees out from under us so that we may deny God and abandon our faith. However, we are encouraged to take shelter in the goodness of God and His purposes.

Resist the lies and temptations of the evil one, for our God is faithful and good. He works out plans to bless and prosper us, ensuring that even in the midst of trials, His ultimate purpose prevails. Let us thank God for His enduring faithfulness throughout our lives and find refuge in His goodness, standing firm against the enticements of the evil one.

Day 71
THE DANGER OF ANGER

"For ships from Cyprus shall come against him; therefore he shall be grieved, and return in rage against the holy covenant, and do damage."

DANIEL 11:30A

IMAGINE a crowded highway, cars zooming past each other in a synchronized dance of motion. Amidst this symphony of movement, two drivers find themselves entangled in a dangerous web of anger and retaliation. A perceived offense ignites the spark, and like a wildfire, anger spreads recklessly, endangering not only the two involved but also those innocent travelers who share the road.

In this analogy, road rage mirrors the dangerous cycle of retaliation that certain kings in Daniel's vision demonstrate. Much like the aggressive driver tailgating another, one such king, feeling the sting of a bitter defeat, turned his rage towards the people of God. Each retaliatory move, fueled by anger, escalated the danger, much like the drivers making increasingly reckless choices on the highway.

As we reflect on this imagery, it's crucial to recognize the parallel in our own lives. How often do we, feeling slighted or hurt, respond in anger and retaliation? The toxic cycle of revenge can spiral out of control, causing harm not only to our relationships but also to those around us.

Luke 6:27-28 serves as a poignant reminder from Jesus Himself: "But I say to you who hear, love your enemies, do good to those who hate you, bless those who curse you, and pray for those who spitefully use you." In the face of injustice, Christ calls us to respond with love, mercy, and prayer. This counter-cultural approach challenges the destructive power of anger and retaliation.

Adding weight to this warning, 1 Thessalonians 5:15 admonishes us: "See that no one renders evil for evil to anyone, but always pursue what is good both for yourselves and for all." The call is clear: resist the urge to repay evil with evil. Instead, respond with love, seeking the well being of others.

Careless anger, much like reckless driving, places our relationships on a perilous path. God, in His wisdom, commands us to care for one another by controlling our anger and countering it with love and grace. As we navigate the highways of life, may we remember that unchecked anger not only endangers our spiritual well-being but also harms those we encounter along the way.

Careless anger places our relationships on a path of reckless danger.

In the midst of provocation, let us pause, breathe, and reflect on the teachings of Christ. Through love, mercy, and prayer, we can break the cycle of anger, bringing healing and restoration to our relationships. May the grace of God empower us to respond to life's afflictions with a spirit of love and understanding, steering clear of the reckless danger that anger and retaliation inevitably bring.

Day 72

SPIRITUAL TREASON

"So he shall return and show regard for those who forsake the holy covenant... and those who do wickedly against the covenant."

DANIEL 11:30B, 32A

COMBAT tales of prisoners of war (POWs) contain the harrowing accounts of men and women trapped in the crucible of conflict. The pressures they face are not merely physical but delve into the recesses of the psychological and emotional realms. The enemy seeks to exploit their weakened state, pressuring them to defect, commit treason, and divulge sensitive information for strategic gain. It's a struggle not just against external pressures, but also against the internal battle to retain loyalty and resilience in the face of overwhelming odds.

In Daniel's vision, we find a parallel to the complex dynamics faced by POWs in the spiritual realm. The nation of Israel, besieged by the relentless persecution of invading kings, encountered immense pressure to forsake their holy covenant with God. The temptations were severe, mirroring the tactics employed on the battlegrounds of war. The promise of a

The call to please God as our commanding officer takes precedence over the entanglements of worldly affairs.

comfortable existence, preservation of life, and relief from hardships led many to commit spiritual treason — forsaking God.

The scenario depicted in Daniel's vision mirrors the spiritual condition prevalent in our world today. The pressures of this world, the trials, persecutions, and hardships, serve as the circumstances in which spiritual loyalties are tested. Jesus, in the parable of the sower, spoke of those whose hearts were like rocky soil — individuals who, lacking deep roots, wither away from God and His truth when faced with the intensity of life's troubles.

In the midst of spiritual conflicts, we are called to be resilient soldiers for Christ. 2 Timothy 2:3-4 emphasizes this point, "Endure hardship with us like a good soldier of Christ Jesus. No one serving as a soldier gets entangled in civilian affairs, but rather tries to please his commanding officer." Despite the pressures to commit spiritual treason, we are exhorted to endure like good soldiers. The call to please God as our commanding officer takes precedence over the entanglements of worldly affairs.

Now, more than ever, is the time to reject the temptations and pressures of this world. It is a time to pledge our unwavering loyalty and dedicated allegiance to the Lord. The path of spiritual resilience is marked by the acknowledgment that we belong to God, that we serve Him, and that He will protect and deliver us from harm as we endure in seeking to please and follow Him.

As we navigate the spiritual battleground of life, may our devotion to God remain unshaken, our commitment unyielding, and our perseverance steadfast. Indeed, the spiritual trials and temptations may be intense, but our God is greater. In the face of adversity, persevere, for His promises are sure — He will strengthen and comfort those who remain faithful to the end.

Day 73
GREAT EXPLOITS

"But the people who know their God shall be strong, and carry out great exploits. And those of the people who understand shall instruct many."

DANIEL 11:32B, 33A

IN the face of danger and uncertainty, emergency first responders demonstrate unparalleled courage and selflessness. Firefighters, paramedics, and law enforcement officers willingly place themselves in harm's way, confronting danger head-on to rescue those in desperate need. Their valiant acts inspire admiration and respect, showcasing a level of commitment and bravery that serves as an analogy for the great exploits described in the book of Daniel.

Much like these modern day heroes, the followers of God depicted in Daniel's vision exemplified heroic and remarkable feats of faith. Daniel 11:32b-33a paints a vivid picture of those who knew their God, declaring them strong and capable of carrying out great exploits. These individuals were not mere spectators of faith but active participants, engaging in extraordinary deeds amid intense trials and persecution. Their exploits went beyond human comprehension, showcasing the supernatural intervention of God in their daily lives.

Daniel speaks not only of personal triumphs, but also of the responsibility to instruct and inspire others. Those who understand and have experienced the faithfulness of God, are called to instruct many. This legacy of faith is not selfishly guarded but generously shared to ignite a flame of boldness and perseverance in others. In the face of persecution and trials, these faithful individuals not only endure, but also teach and encourage others to follow their example.

Today, as followers of Christ, we are called to embrace a similar spirit of daring faith. Jesus, in John 14:10, encourages His disciples with the promise that they will do great works for God because they trust in Him. Ephesians 3:20 reinforces this truth, assuring us that God's power working within us can accomplish extraordinary things beyond our wildest imagination. In light of these promises, we are reminded that any great work of God through us begins and ends with the mighty power of God present in us.

Any great work of God through us begins and ends with the mighty power of God present in us.

Even in our moments of perceived weakness, God's power is more than sufficient to accomplish His good, pleasing, and perfect will in our lives. Let us commit to bravely serving God, following the example of those who carried out great exploits in the past. May we humbly lead people to Him, inspired by the heroic feats of faith displayed by those who knew their God. In doing so, we trust that God's power will work in us to achieve His purposes, and through us, He will continue to accomplish extraordinary things for His glory.

Day 74

PURPOSE IN THE PAIN

> "And some of those of understanding shall fall, to refine them, purify them, and make them white, until the time of the end."
>
> **DANIEL 11:35**

LIFE often resembles the process of making diamonds. These rare, beautiful, and enduring gems are formed under immense pressure and heat over extended periods – making them precious and highly valuable. In a similar way, Daniel 11:35 paints a vivid picture of the spiritual journey, describing a refining process that purifies and makes God's people white. The analogy of diamonds serves as a powerful metaphor for understanding the purpose in our pain and trials.

Daniel's vision looked forward to a time of intense persecution for followers of God, where some would even pay the ultimate sacrifice as martyrs. It's a glimpse into a reality where the magnitude of suffering tests the mettle of one's faith. Just as carbon transforms into diamonds under pressure, so too our lives are shaped and refined through the intense trials we face.

We can only cheer for the trials when we cherish the trade-off.

Romans 5:3-4 reinforces this perspective: "And not only that, but we also glory in tribulations, knowing that tribulation produces perseverance; and perseverance, character; and character, hope." Every trial we encounter is a step in a divine process that molds our character, strengthens our trust in God, and ultimately forms genuine faith.

In 1 Peter 1:6-7, we find a similar sentiment: "In this you greatly rejoice, though now for a little while, if need be, you have been grieved by various trials, that the genuineness of your faith, being much more precious than gold that perishes, though it is tested by fire, may be found to praise, honor, and glory at the revelation of Jesus Christ."

These verses remind us that our trials are not meaningless; they are purposeful. Just as diamonds are refined by intense pressure and heat, our faith is purified by the trials we face. Though we may experience temporary grief, we are invited to embrace trials with joy, recognizing the enduring faith that is forged in the fires of suffering is more valuable than any earthly treasure.

Understanding God's purpose for pain is transformative. It shifts our perspective, allowing us not only to endure trials, but also to cheer for them when we consider the trade-off: genuine faith refined in the intense pressure and heat of suffering. So, don't give up. Godly patience in trials does not tap out or quit; it sticks it out for the beautiful payoff.

Remember, every trial by fire is a test of faith. Just as diamonds emerge from the rough, let your faith shine brightly through the refining fires. Trust that God, the Master Jeweler, is at work, crafting something beautiful and enduring within you. In the pressures of trials, remember that you are not alone, for God's purpose in your pain is to refine, purify, and make your faith shine like precious and valuable diamonds.

Day 75

KEEP ON, KEEPING ON

"And there shall be a time of trouble, such as never was since there was a nation, even to that time."

DANIEL 12:1

IN the world of marathon running, there exists a remarkable display of diligence, determination, and dedication. Picture the marathon runner, training tirelessly, pushing past limits, enduring grueling pain, all with one singular focus: crossing the finish line. They understand that success demands more than physical prowess; it requires mental fortitude, an unwavering resolve to persevere through the toughest of challenges.

We must carry on with diligence until the coming of Jesus' appearance.

Likewise, as followers of Christ, we are called to embody this same spirit of endurance, especially as we navigate the tumultuous terrain of the end times. In Daniel 12:1, we are forewarned of a time of trouble unparalleled in history. It is described as a period so intense that it surpasses any previous tribulation known to humanity.

Just as the marathon runner faces exhaustion and pain, so too shall we encounter trials that test the very essence of our faith. The prophetic vision of Daniel speaks of persecution and chaos, a time when staying steadfast in our devotion to the Lord will require unyielding perseverance.

Jesus Himself validated Daniel's vision when He foretold similar events to His disciples. In Matthew 24:14, He says, "And this gospel of the kingdom will be preached in all the world as a witness to all nations, and then the end will come." The instruction for us to preach the gospel to all nations, emphasizes the urgency of our mission in the face of impending adversity. We are warned not to be deceived but to remain vigilant and prayerful.

Amidst the apostasy, anarchy, and apathy that characterize the end times, we are called to be faithful stewards of the gospel. Despite the darkness that envelops the world, the light of the gospel shines even brighter. The advancing kingdom of God will not be thwarted by opposition; it will triumph victoriously.

Therefore, let us take heart and press on with diligence until the appearing of our Lord Jesus Christ. Just as the marathon runner keeps focused on the finish line, so too must we fix our eyes on Jesus, the author and finisher of our faith. We must carry on with unwavering determination, knowing that our labor in the Lord is not in vain.

As the world grows darker, let us shine brighter. Let us proclaim the gospel boldly, knowing that our reward awaits us at the end of the race. Keep on, keeping on until the coming of Jesus' appearance, for in Him, our hope is secure, and our victory is assured.

Day 76
RESURRECTION POWER

"And many of those who sleep in the dust of the earth shall awake, some to everlasting life, some to shame and everlasting contempt."

DANIEL 12:2

CONSIDER a seed, fallen from a mighty tree, lying dormant in the earth. Buried beneath the surface, it seems lifeless, surrounded by darkness. Yet, when the conditions align – water, nutrients, and sunlight – this seemingly lifeless seed bursts forth, breaking the shackles of dormancy, heralding the arrival of new life. This cycle of life wonderfully illustrates the powerful transformation of the resurrection.

In Daniel's vision, God granted insight into future prophetic events: the rise and fall of the final world dictator, the great battle of Armageddon, the events of the great tribulation, the return of Jesus, and the resurrection of the dead. It's a vision of cosmic proportions, a glimpse into the unfolding drama of God's redemptive plan.

Just as the seed undergoes a transformation, our bodies too will experience a resurrection. Daniel speaks of those who sleep in the dust and will awaken: some to everlasting life and others to shame and contempt. The imagery describes the resurrection of the dead. This echoes the biblical truth that our physical bodies will perish, but our souls are immortal. Our souls are precious and valuable to God, beyond any earthly measure.

The verses in Daniel guide us to a moment when we stand before a just and holy God. A time when the righteous — those whose sins have been washed by the blood of the Lamb — receive the reward of eternal life; and those who reject God's salvation through Jesus face eternal separation. Our souls are at the center of this divine transaction, and there is nothing in this world that compares to their worth.

The resurrection is the promise that death in Christ springs forth into everlasting life.

The great truth of John 11:25 echoes through the ages: "I am the resurrection and the life. He who believes in Me, though he may die, he shall live." Jesus, through His resurrection, imparts this same resurrection power to us. It's a power that breaks the chains of sin and conquers the grip of death. Through faith in Christ, we receive victory over the grave. The resurrection is the promise that death in Christ springs forth into everlasting life.

Remarkably, it is God's desire that none should perish, and so He gave us Jesus — a gift of love for the forgiveness of sins and the reconciliation of our relationship with God. As we ponder these truths, we are compelled to examine our hearts and respond to the Savior's call.

As you reflect on Daniel's vision and the resurrection power embedded in it, consider your response before God. The promise of resurrection power beckons us to ensure our sins are washed and cleansed through faith in Jesus. Through Him, we find assurance that, just like the seed, we will experience new life, vibrant and eternal, in the presence of our resurrected Lord.

Day 77

LIGHT THE NIGHT

"Those who are wise shall shine like the brightness of the firmament, and those who turn many to righteousness like the stars forever and ever."

DANIEL 12:3

IN the vast expanse of the night sky, the stars emerge with a brilliance that captivates our gaze. Each one, a shimmering beacon of light, radiating beauty and splendor that cuts through the darkness. The celestial cosmos, adorned with unique constellations, paints a portrait of majestic twinkles that draw our eyes upwards in awe. These stars not only illuminate the night but also serve as guides, helping explorers navigate courses and plot paths across uncharted seas and wild terrains.

Much like the stars in the heavens, followers of God are called to shine with a brilliance that pierces the darkness of this world. Daniel, in his vision, was granted a glimpse into the future where those who walk in the wisdom of God are promised a reward for their faithfulness on earth. These wise individuals are described as shining like the brightness of the firmament, radiating light that leads others to righteousness.

Consider the stars, they do not hoard their light, but generously share it with the world. Likewise, as disciples of Christ, we are called to use our time, talent, and treasures to glorify God and point people to the Lord through our words and actions. Jesus, in Matthew 5:14-16 affirms this, declaring, "You are the light of the world. Don't hide your light, but let your light so shine before men, that they may see your good works and glorify your Father in heaven."

Jesus has given us His light to reflect and radiate through our actions. We are, in a sense, the stars of His creation, strategically placed to illuminate the darkness and guide others to the true source of light and life. This truth reminds us of the eternal perspective that it is worth every second to invest our lives in things that last forever.

In a world filled with uncertainty and darkness, our lives can be a beacon of hope. We are called to live in wisdom, utilizing every opportunity to share the love and grace of Christ. As we navigate the journey of life, may our actions reflect the brilliant light of our Savior, guiding others to the God of hope in the midst of a dark and desperate world.

In the end, it is not the temporal pursuits that matter most, but the eternal impact of our lives on those around us.

So, how is your light shining for Jesus? Are you wisely investing your time now with eternity in mind? Take a moment to reflect on your life. Are you leveraging every opportunity to walk in the wisdom of God's truth? Determine today to live in such a way that you glorify God and light the way for others to find hope and purpose. In the end, it is not the temporal pursuits that matter most, but the eternal impact of our lives on those around us.

Day 78

CALL UPON THE LORD

"Although I heard, I did not understand. Then I said, 'What shall be the end of these things.'"

DANIEL 12:8

IN the exhilarating game show "Who Wants to Be a Millionaire?" contestants face a cascade of questions, each more challenging than the last, with the allure of a million-dollar prize hanging in the balance. To aid them on this quest, they are granted lifelines, one of which is aptly named "phone-a-friend." When the going gets tough, contestants can call upon a friend for assistance, tapping into an external source of knowledge to help overcome the challenge before them.

Daniel, a man gifted with extraordinary wisdom and understanding of prophetic visions, found himself in a similar predicament. In the midst of profound visions, he encountered aspects that left him perplexed and seeking clarity. Despite his remarkable insights, Daniel acknowledged that there were elements beyond his comprehension, prompting him to say, "Although I heard, I do not understand."

Our God is not a distant force but an ever-present Friend waiting for our call.

Even in our spiritual journey, filled with moments of revelation and understanding, there will be parts of God's Word and His ways that may leave us puzzled. As we delve into the Scriptures or navigate the intricate pathways of life, there may be seasons of confusion or aspects not entirely clear. Just like the contestants on the game show, we encounter questions that seem beyond our understanding.

Yet, the beauty lies not in our ability to unravel every mystery, but in our aid of the ultimate lifeline: calling upon the Lord. Jeremiah 33:3 extends to us a powerful invitation with a profound promise, a divine phone-a-friend lifeline from God: "Call to Me, and I will answer you, and show you great and mighty things, which you do not know."

Our God is not a distant force but an ever-present Friend waiting for our call. In times of uncertainty and confusion, we are encouraged to lift our hearts in prayer, reaching out to the God of infinite knowledge. He hears our requests, not with the limitations of human understanding, but with the ultimate wisdom that transcends our comprehension.

When faced with questions beyond our capabilities or challenges that seem insurmountable, let us remember that we have a Friend who is always ready to listen. We can approach Him in prayer, confident that He not only hears but responds with divine counsel that transcends our understanding.

So, the next time you find yourself stumped by the questions of life, call upon the Lord. Approach Him as a close friend in prayer, laying before Him your uncertainties and seeking His guidance. In the midst of confusion, God promises to provide clarity. Trust in His infinite wisdom, for He is the answer to the questions that perplex us, and His understanding surpasses all.

Day 79

HEED THE HOLY SPIRIT

"Many shall be purified, made white, and refined, but the wicked shall do wickedly."

DANIEL 12:10

IN the realm of organized and professional sports, there exists a vital component ensuring the integrity of the game: referees, umpires, and officials. These individuals possess a profound understanding of the rules governing the sport they oversee. Their role is not merely ceremonial; rather, they serve as enforcers of order amidst the chaos of competition.

Referees stand as impartial arbiters, ensuring that players adhere to the rules set forth. Their discernment prevents the eruption of disorder and maintains the fairness essential to the game's essence. Much like these officials, the Holy Spirit acts as a spiritual referee in our lives, guiding us in accordance with God's divine standards.

The Holy Spirit's responsibility is to reveal immorality.

Towards the close of the book of Daniel, amidst prophetic visions of the end times, we encounter a stark warning of the future tragic condition of the human heart. Daniel's vision portrays a world divided between those who embrace holiness and righteousness and those who willfully persist in wickedness and rebellion. It foretells a period where moral decay will proliferate, and humanity will prioritize personal pleasure over pleasing God.

The New Testament corroborates this vision, describing a time of unprecedented lawlessness and division. In 2 Thessalonians 2:7, it is written: "For the mystery of lawlessness is already at work; only He who now restrains will do so until He is taken out of the way." Here, we find assurance that amidst the rebellion, the Holy Spirit remains actively engaged, restraining immorality and convicting hearts towards righteousness.

The Holy Spirit reveals immorality, much like a referee calling fouls on the field. His presence in the world and in our lives serves as a compass — pointing out truth and exposing areas where we've strayed from God's Word. Just as players heed the calls of officials to avoid penalties, we are called to heed the promptings of the Holy Spirit, aligning our lives with God's precepts.

In a world where wickedness abounds and the allure of sin beckons, it is imperative that we remain sensitive to the Holy Spirit's guidance. His conviction redirects our focus towards righteousness, guiding us along the path of obedience and holiness. As players in the game of life, we must heed the Holy Spirit's calls, striving to please God and live according to His ways.

Let us not be swayed by the tide of lawlessness or the pursuit of selfish desires. Instead, may we yield to the gentle promptings of the Holy Spirit, allowing Him to purify and refine our hearts. In doing so, we embody the righteousness foretold by Daniel and become bright lights in a darkened world.

Day 80
ENTER GOD'S REST

"But you, go your way till the end; for you shall rest, and will arise to your inheritance at the end of the days."

DANIEL 12:13

THE book of Psalms stands out as a magnificent collection of Hebrew poetry, resonating with beautiful cadence and eloquent inspiration. Each psalm is a melodious composition, carefully crafted as songs to the Lord. One recurring feature of these poetic masterpieces is the word "Selah." This term signals a melodic break — a momentary pause in the music for a reflective interlude. These serene intermissions provide moments of silence, a sacred hush to rest and reflect on the goodness of God.

Much like these intentional pauses in the Psalms, our lives are marked by seasons requiring a pause — a break from the constant demands of daily tasks, worries, and pursuits. In the busyness of life, it becomes crucial for us to find those Selah moments of respite, peaceful soothing intervals of silence to rest and reflect on the majesty and faithfulness of our Creator.

Consider the life of Daniel, a faithful servant of the Lord whose story is woven with threads of spiritual bravery and courageous faith. From his youthful days in Babylon to his role as a counselor to powerful kings in the Persian Empire, Daniel's life was a testament to his unwavering commitment to God. In his later years, Daniel received and recorded prophetic visions, a divine encore to a life lived in service to the Almighty.

Approaching the end of his earthly pilgrimage, Daniel's life reflects the promise of God's rest and eternal inheritance. Similarly, in Matthew 25:21 Jesus speaks of the joy awaiting those who have been faithful stewards: "Well done, good and faithful servant, enter into the joy of your lord." Daniel's life was marked by loyalty to the Lord, spiritual integrity, and submission to the sovereignty of God. His example points to the future promise where faithful servants are rewarded for their fidelity and fruitful labor.

Daniel's life invites us to consider the importance of pauses in our own journey. In the midst of life's busyness, we are called to take moments to rest in the peace and presence of the Lord. These pauses allow us to reflect on God's goodness, seek His guidance, and find rejuvenation for our weary souls.

Spiritual pauses allow us to reflect on God's goodness, seek His guidance, and find rejuvenation for our weary souls.

As we navigate the symphony of life, let us heed the rhythmic call of the Psalms — a call to pause, to reflect, and to find rest in the peace and presence of the Lord. Take comfort in the assurance that there is an ultimate spiritual rest for our souls and an eternal inheritance awaiting those who remain faithful and walk humbly with God. May the divine Selahs in our lives be moments of respite, guiding us to enter God's rest and inherit the promises reserved for the faithful.

Quest Ministries

Connect with us online

QuestSd.com
@ourquestsd
info@questsd.com

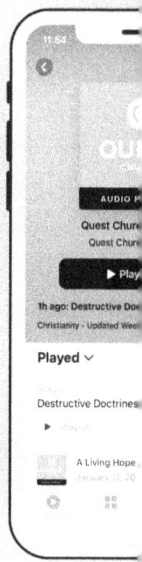

www.ingramcontent.com/pod-product-compliance
Lightning Source LLC
Chambersburg PA
CBHW050907160426
43194CB00011B/2320